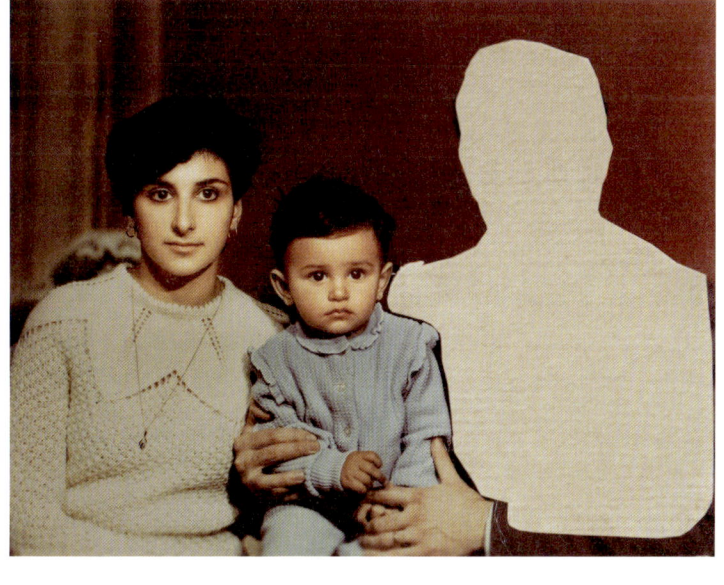

Father

Diana Markosian

aperture

For my brother, David,
who became a father to me

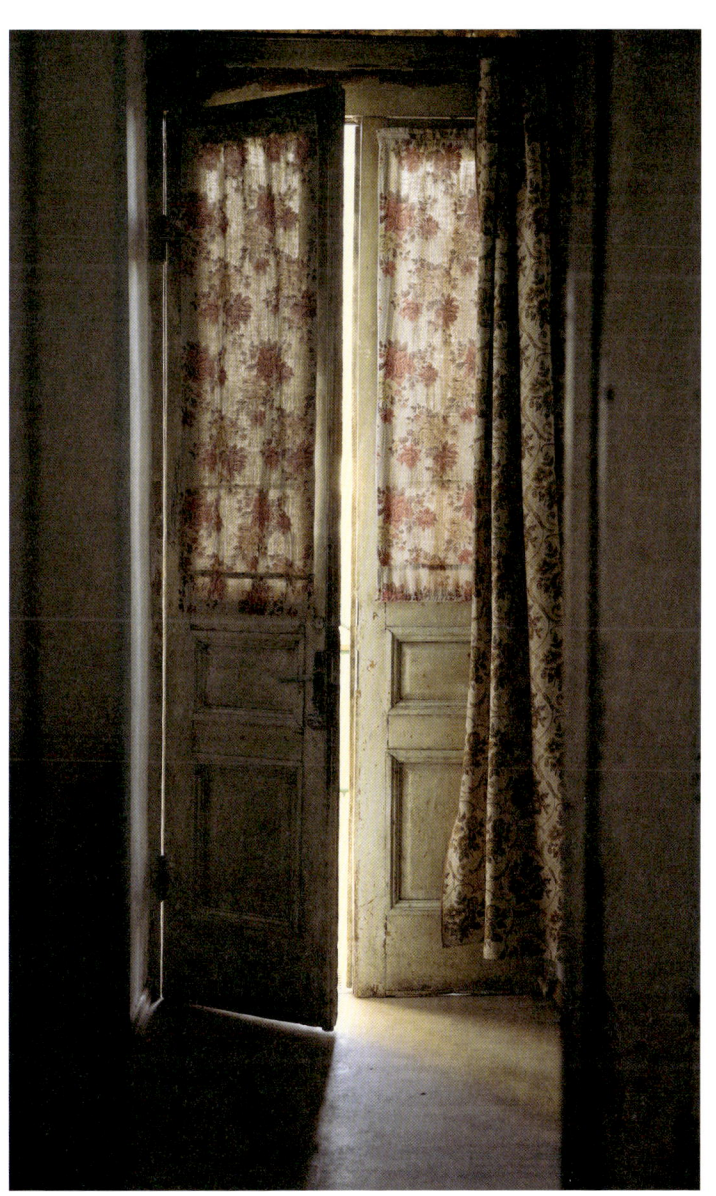

For most of my life, my father was nothing more
than a silhouette in our family album.

When I was seven,
my mother woke my brother and me in our apartment
in Moscow and told us to pack our belongings.
We didn't say goodbye to my father.

The next morning, we arrived in California.
I didn't understand it then, but it would be our new home.
For my mom, the way to forget my father was simple.
She cut his image out of every family photograph.
For me, those holes made it harder to forget him.

In America, I waited for him to come find me.
He never did.
I often wondered what it would have been like to have a father.
I still do.

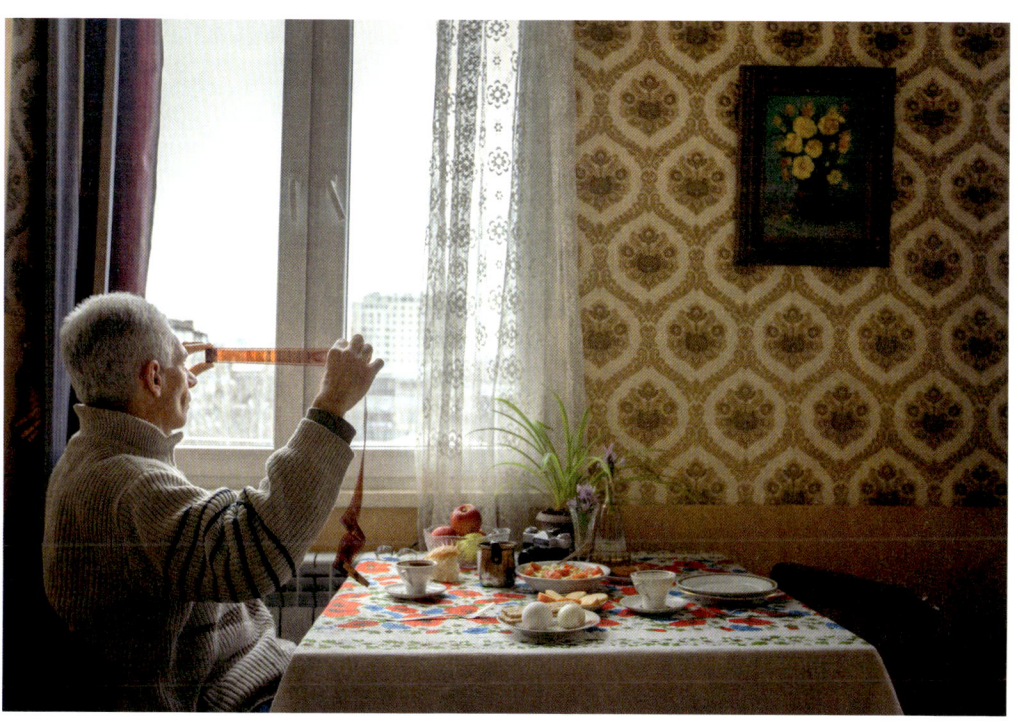

I have only a few memories of my father.
In one, we're dancing together.
In another, he's walking out of our apartment.

My parents were separated before I was born.
My father would often visit.
Today I am the visitor.
I haven't seen him since I was seven.

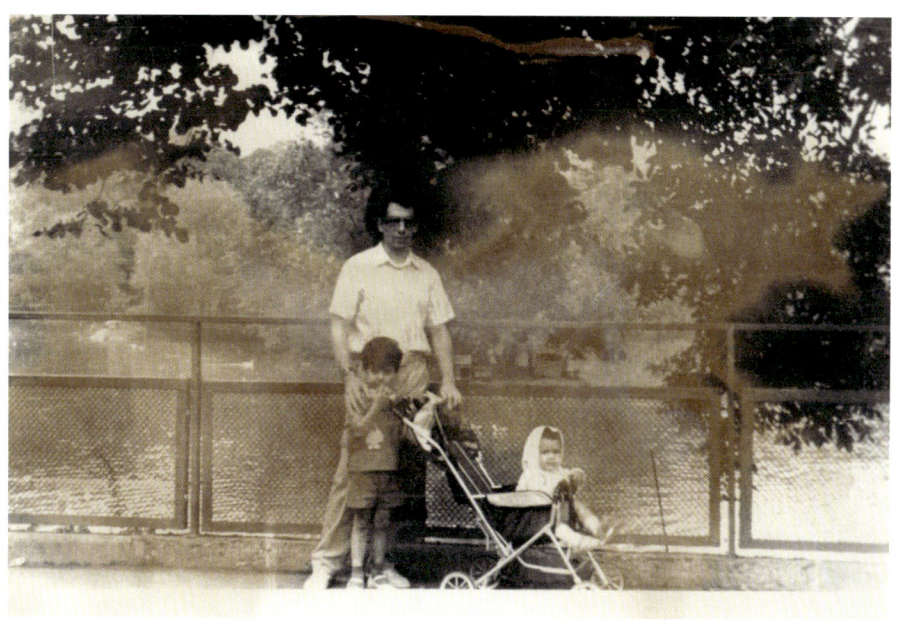

I am in the courtyard outside his apartment.
I can't recall what he looks like.

As a kid, I tried to ask my mother about him.
"I am forgetting his eyes," I said.
"Good," she replied. "I forgot them a long time ago."

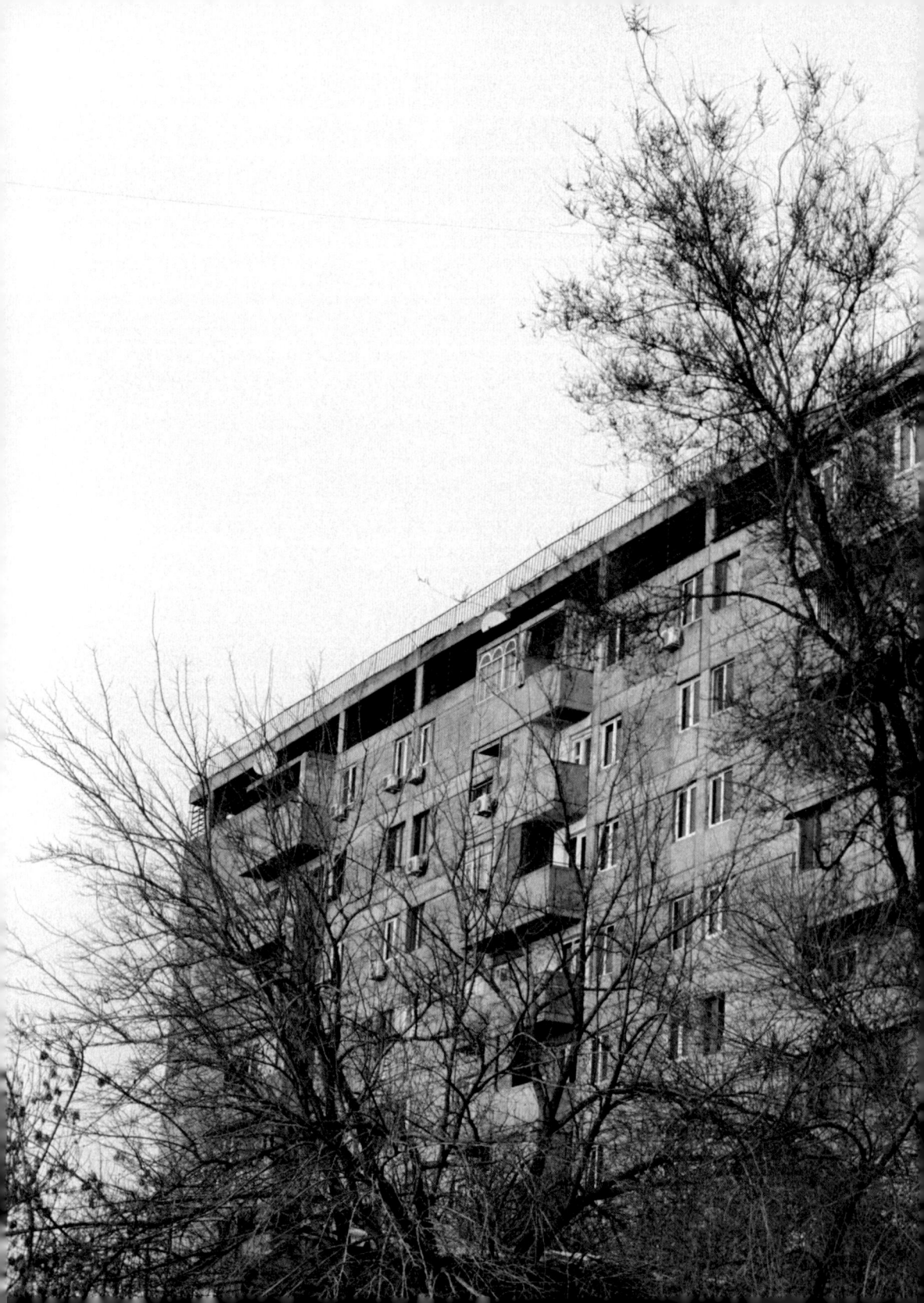

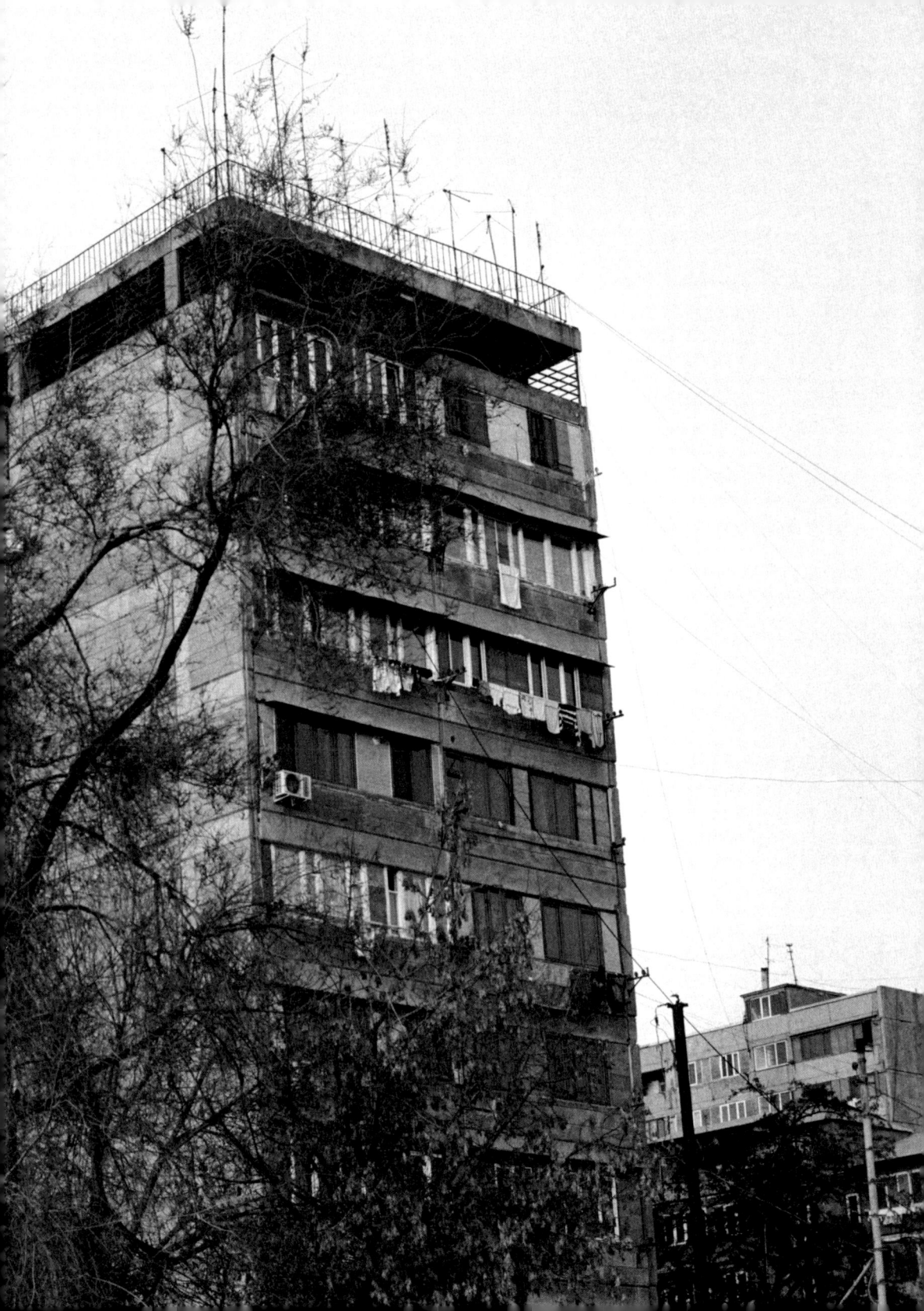

I knock on his door.
It's been 15 years.
"Can I help you?" a man asks.
"I am Diana, your daughter."

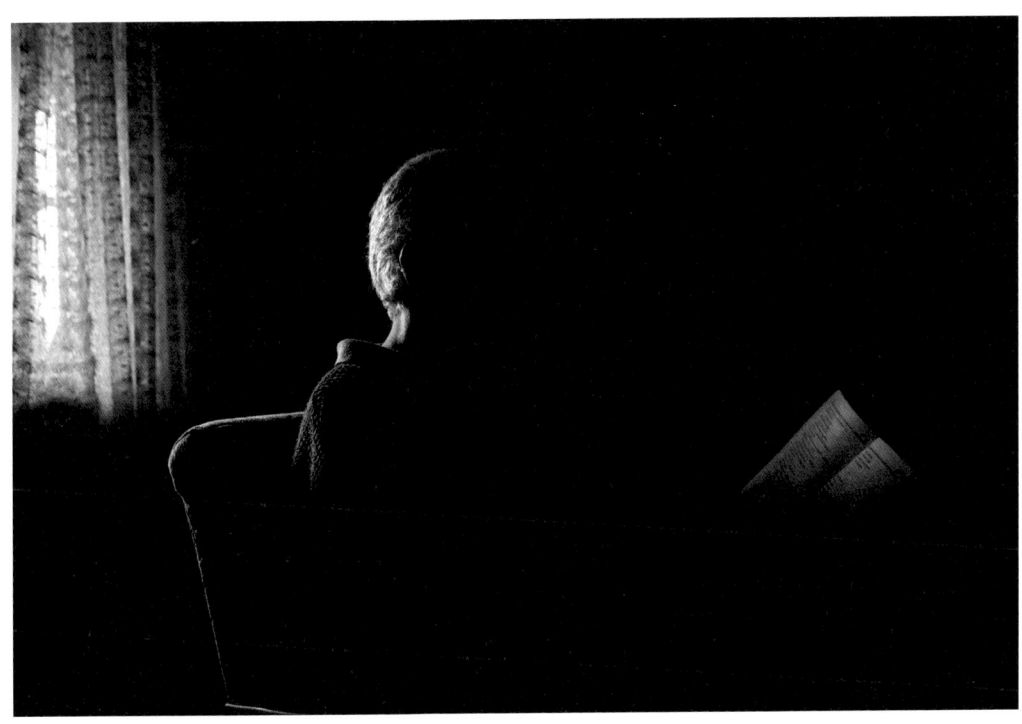

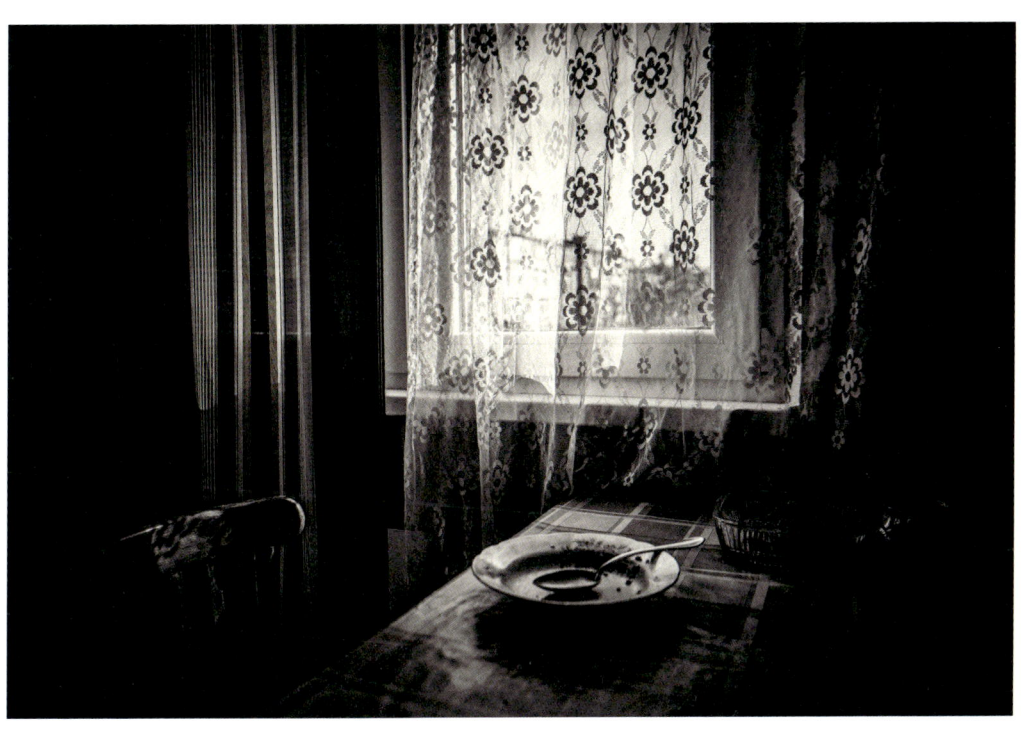

His hair is gray.
His face is gaunt.
His shoulders are slumped.

At first, he doesn't recognize me.
I don't recognize him either.

"Why did it take you so long?" he asks.

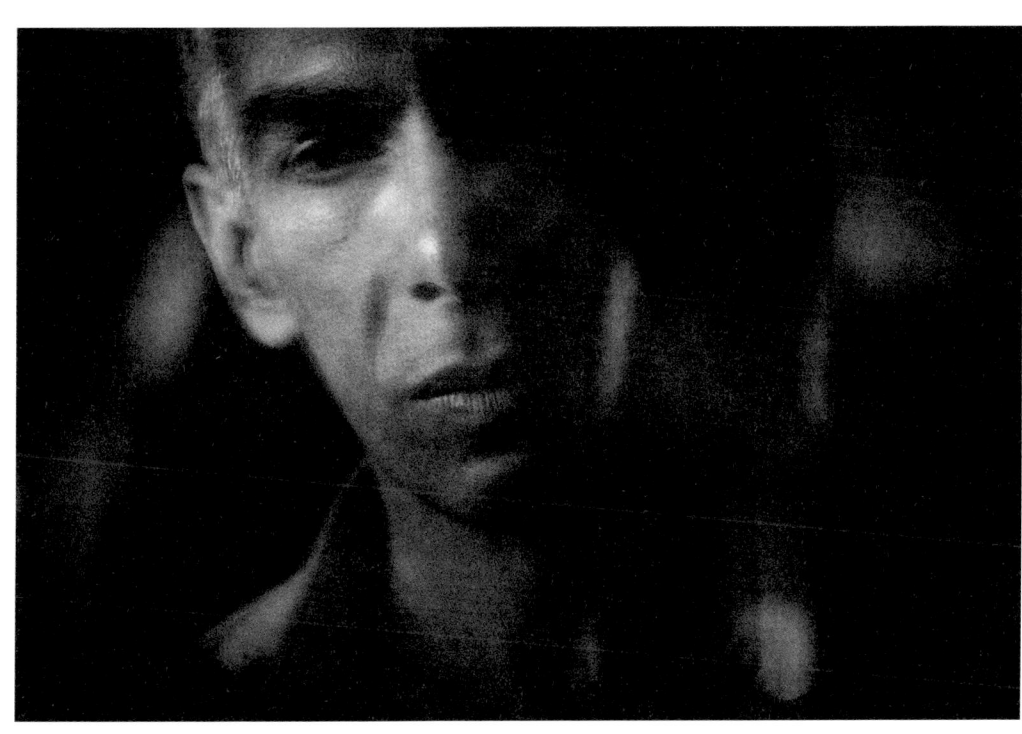

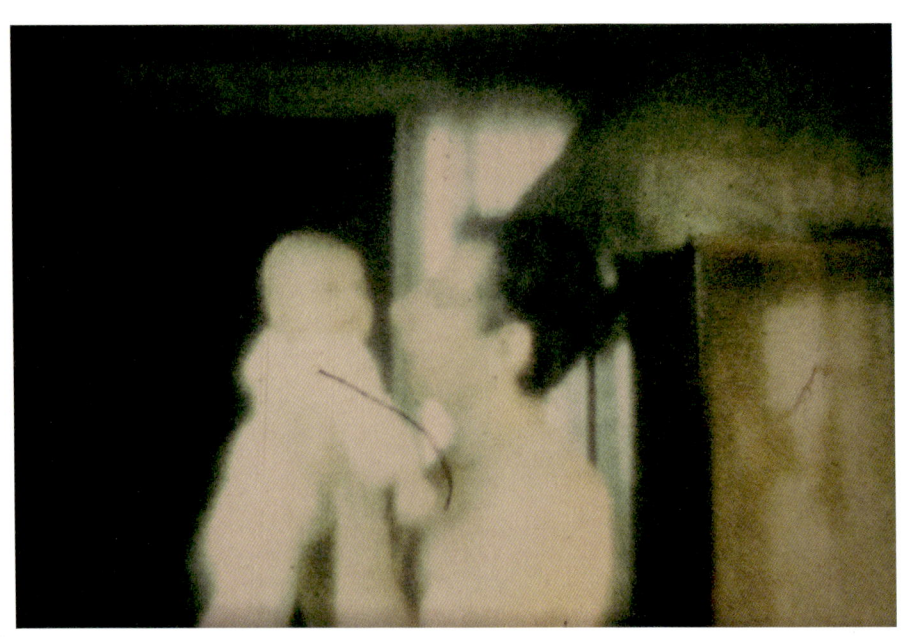

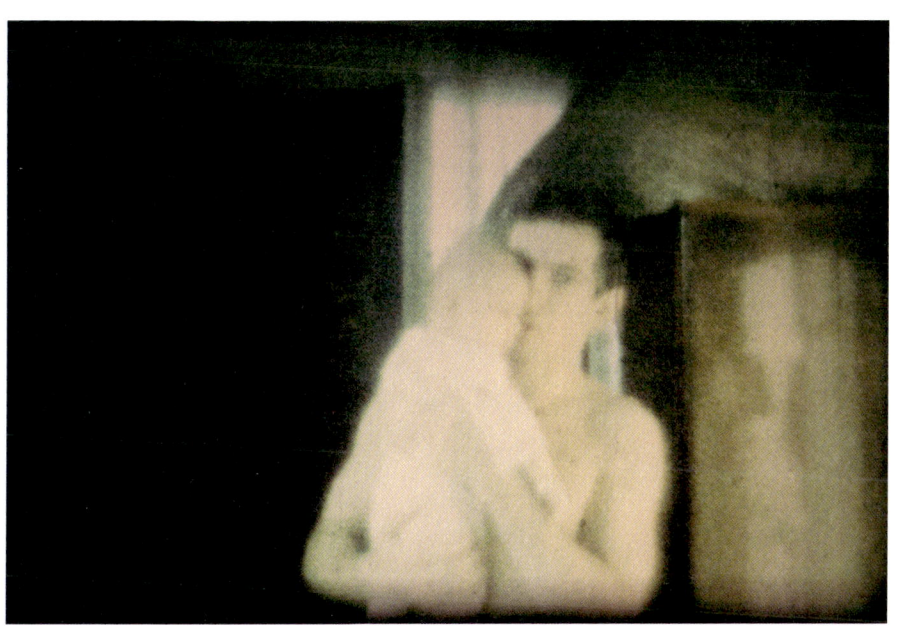

He invites me in.
His home is a museum of my childhood.
My grandfather's oil paintings and our family pictures decorate the walls.
Polka-dot tins line the kitchen shelves.
A closet stores my brother's childhood toys.

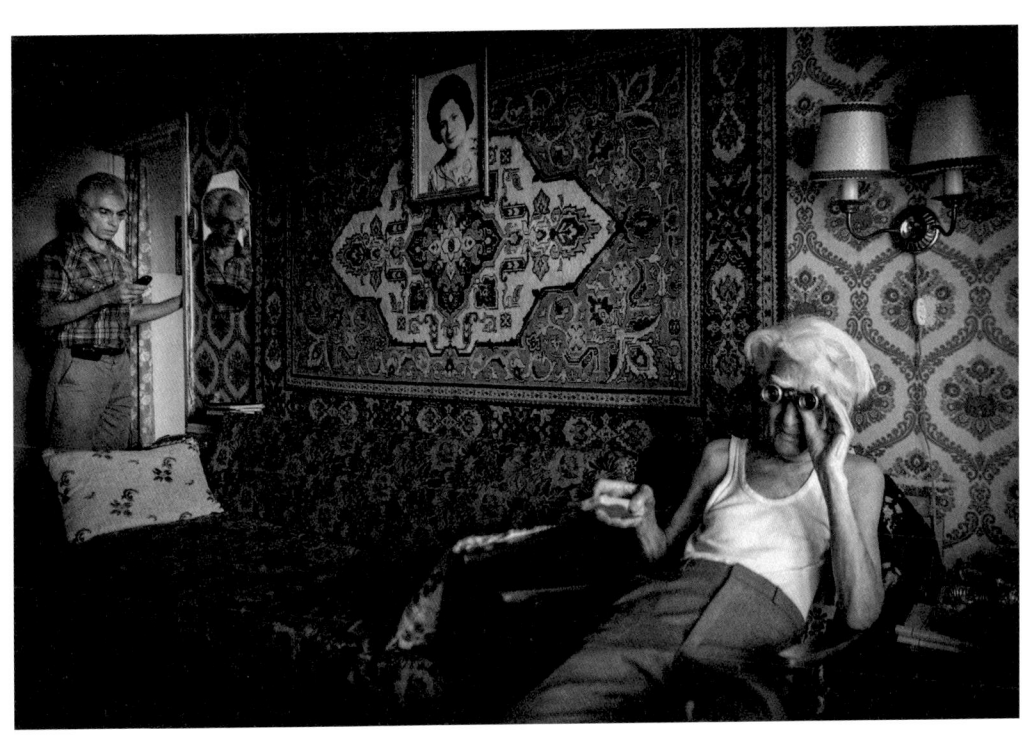

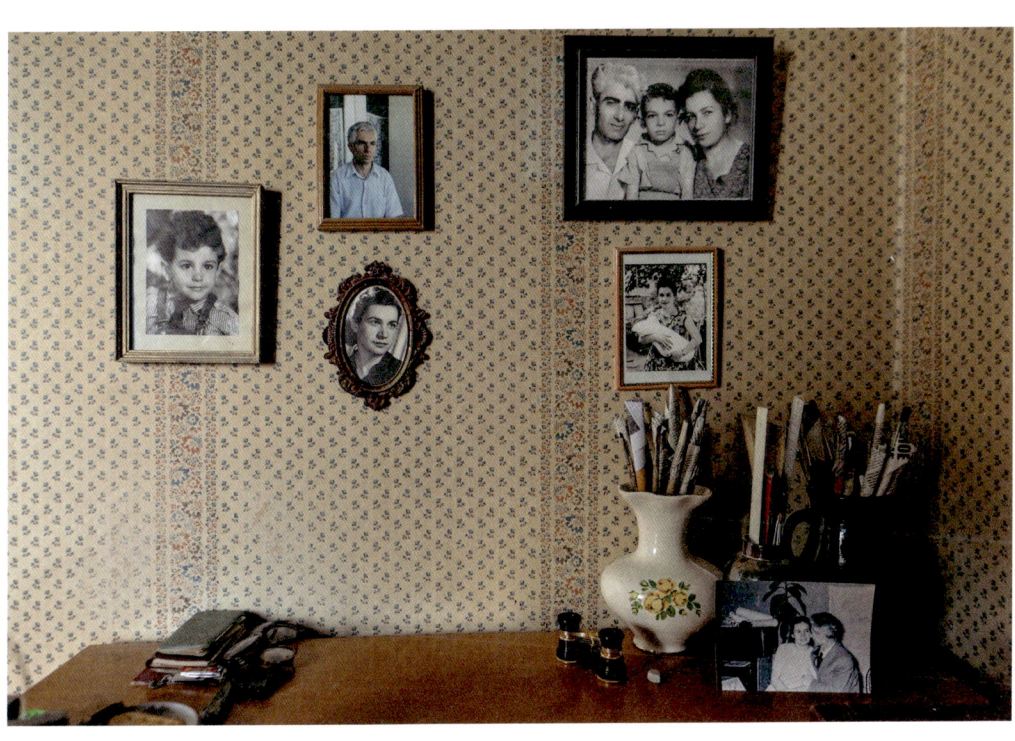

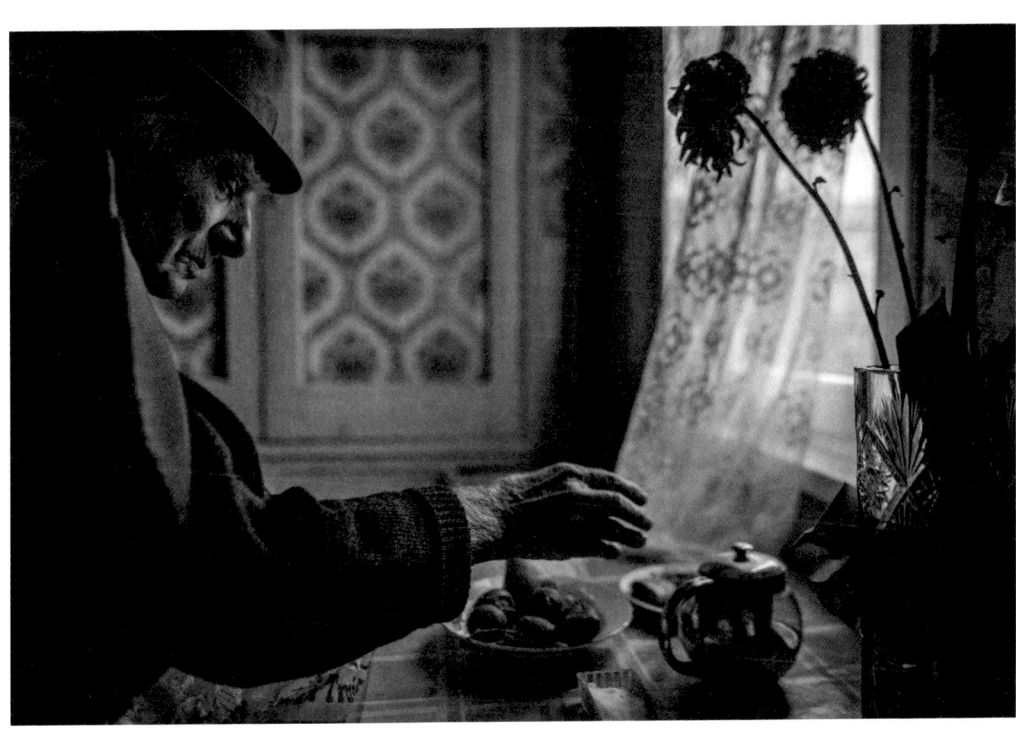

He says he has been looking for me.
He opens a suitcase.
Inside, a shirt for my brother's future wedding
and a collection of books for me.
Beneath them, hundreds of letters he wrote,
searching for us.
A newspaper clipping with my photo, the words
missing child printed over it.

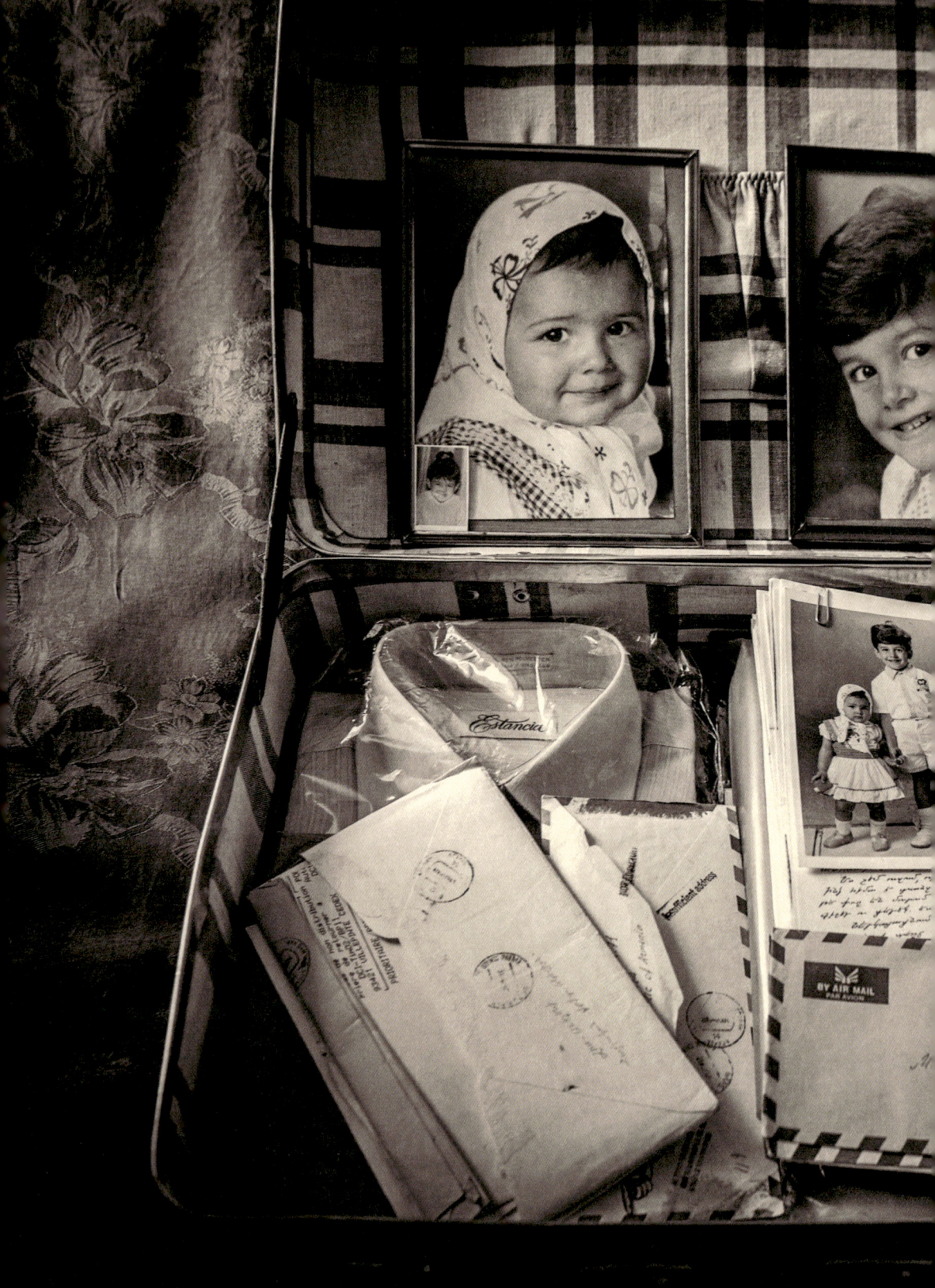

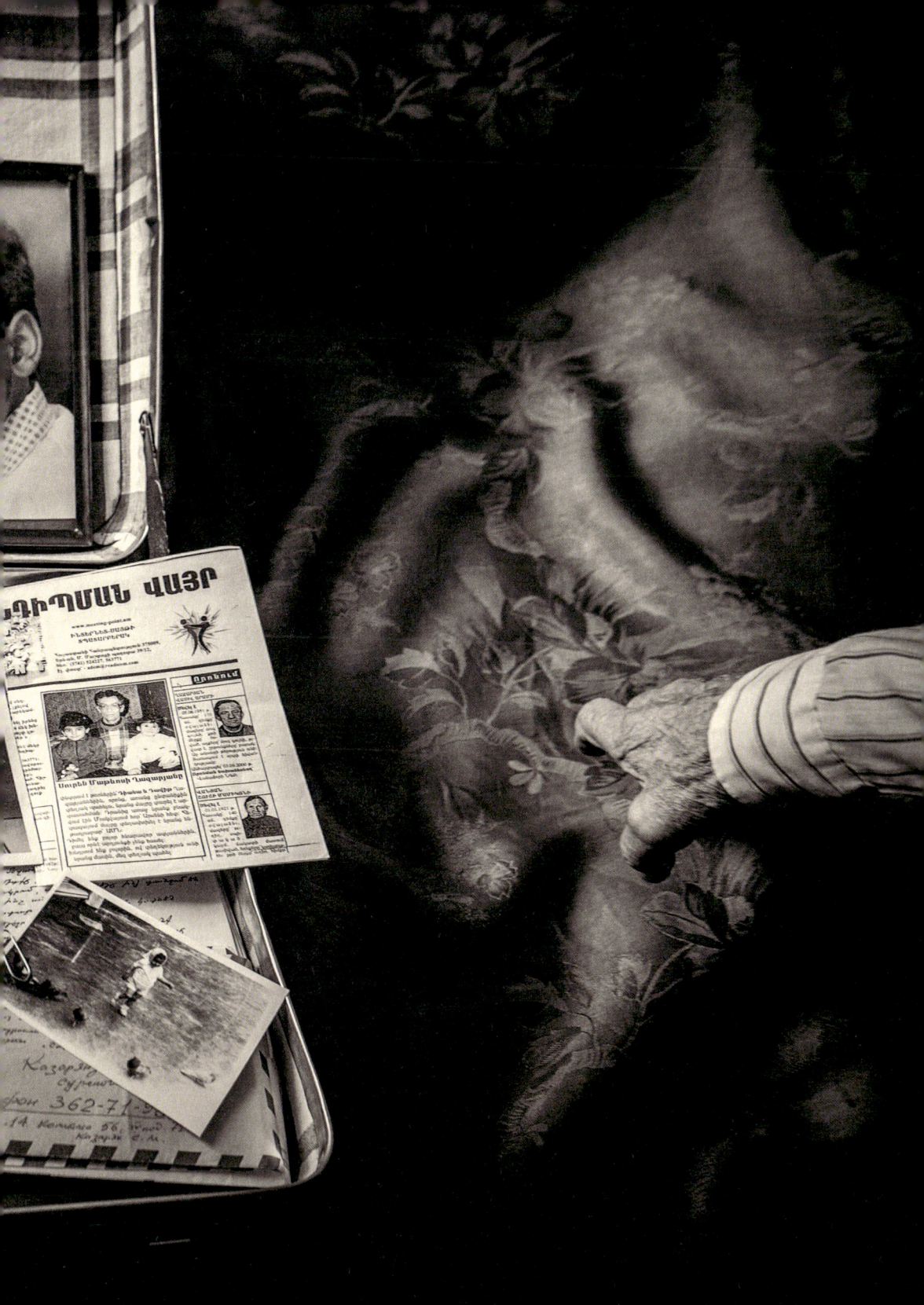

ТОЧКА ВСТРЕЧИ

ПРИНТ-ВЕРСИЯ ПОИСКОВОГО
ИНТЕРНЕТ-САЙТА

www.meeting-point.am

Адрес: Республика Армения, 375009,
Ереван, пр. М.Маштоца, 39/12

Тел.: (3741) 524227, 563771

Электронная почта: adem@readcom.am

Институт Открытого
Фонд С...
Армянский...
Центр ...

ВЫПУСК

MEETING POI

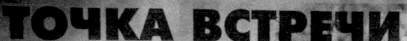

Судьба армянского народа сложилась так, что армяне оказались разбросанными по всему миру. Особенно внушительных размеров последняя волна миграции достигла в прошедшие десять-пятнадцать лет. Люди, покидавшие места обитания в экстремальных условиях, часто теряли из поля зрения своих родных и близких, друзей и коллег. Заброшенные событиями в разные страны, они часто даже не представляют, где могут находиться друзья и родственники, каковы их судьбы. Еще одна сторона проблемы – без вести пропавшие. По данным МВД, только в Армении ежегодно пропадает несколько десятков человек. Большое количество армянских фамилий числится в списках без вести пропавших в России и других странах СНГ.

Надеемся, что в поиске этих людей поможет наш сайт. Если кто-то располагает сведениями о разыскиваемых людях, просим сообщить эту информацию администрации сайта «Точка встречи» по электронной почте adem@readcom.am или по телефонам (3741) 524227, 563771.

Вниманию тех, кто не имеет доступа в Интернет, мы предлагаем данную принт-версию сайта. Принт-версия выходит каждую последнюю среду (а не пятницу, как ранее сообщалось) месяца как приложение к газетам "Республика Армения" и "Айастани Анрапетутюн". Напоминаем: по адресу Ереван, пр. М. Маштоца, 39/12 действует общественная приемная, где наши специалисты помогут вам провести поиск в Интернете, разместить на сайте объявления о поиске людей и событиях, о которых вы хотели бы известить живущих в других странах и регионах родных и близких.

Казарян Сурен Матевосович

Ищет внуков – Диану и Давида Казарянов, которых увезла за рубеж без ведома семьи их мать. Они вначале проживали в Москве с отцом Арменом, однако затем мать увезла детей, предположительно, в США. Обращения во все возможные инстанции результатов не дали. Просьба ко всем, кто что-либо знает, дать знать.

Поиск

Тумасян Карине

Родилась в г. Баку, работала на заводе в поселке Лок-Батан. В 90-е годы, после известных бакинских событий, переехала в Ереван.
Ищет: Бакинцы, проживающие в Москве.

Тадевосян Карлен

Родился в Азербайджане, Баку.

ресу – USA 1842 N.WILTON # L/A Calif90028
Регион поиска: США.
Ищет: Каградзарян Карине

Апроян Арамаис Аршевович

Родился в 1907 г. в Армении (пор Бигаия Нами). Его брат отец. С 1942 участвовал в Великой Отечественной войне. В Армении было 4 зам. В 50-х годах поиски открытия из-за рубежа. Его адрес (оэной номер) не дан. Может быть, он был в Грузии. Была его семья и дети.

"My children are gone," he wrote the year we disappeared.
That was 1996.
"Their mother secretly took them to America.
Please write if you have any information."
Every year, my father and grandfather wrote letters to embassies,
police stations, toy stores, and random American addresses
they found in newspapers.
The letters never reached us.

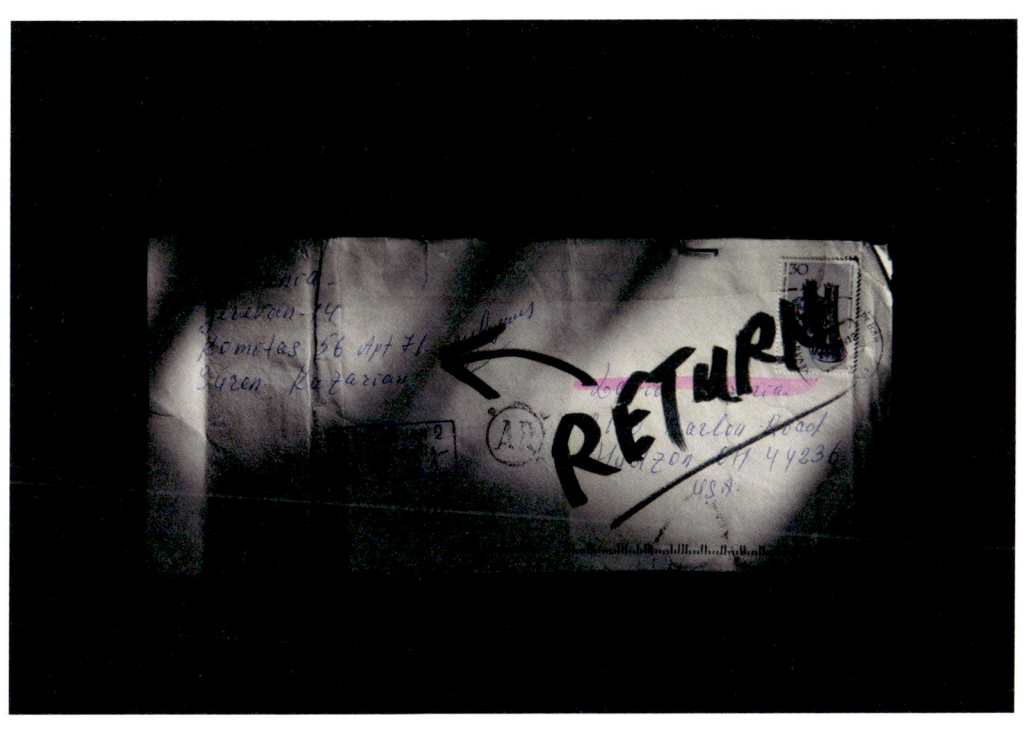

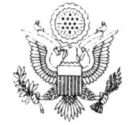

Moscow, Russia
March 19, 1997

Mr. ░░░░░░░░░░
P. O. Box 71
Moscow, 111020

Dear Mr. ░░░░░░ :

I am writing in response to your recent letter, which we received here on February 5, 1997, regarding the whereabouts of your wife, Mrs. Svetlana ░░░░░░░░░░░░░░░░░ , your son, David, and your daughter, Diana. In your letter, you indicated that you believe that Mrs. Svetlana ░░░░░ relocated to the United States in 1996 together with your children without notifying you. In this regard, you requested that we convey to you information concerning Mrs. Svetlana ░░░░░ 's whereabouts and status.

The United States Government does not maintain information about the whereabouts of individuals who have immigrated to the U.S. or have entered the U.S. temporarily and decided to remain there illegally or legally. However, we have a record on our file that we issued nonimmigrant visas to your family members on June 21, 1996. Since you believe that they may have settled illegally in Los Angeles, California, I suggest that you consider contacting a local office of the United States Immigration and Naturalization Service for any record they may have on this matter. Below is the INS District office's address in Los Angeles:

300 North Los Angeles St.
Los Angeles, CA 90012

Please, be advised that your letter must be in English. Alternatively, you may wish to hire a private investigator to assist you in this matter. I regret that my response cannot be more forthcoming. Nevertheless, I hope that you find this information helpful.

Sincerely,

Michael W. Marine
Minister Counselor
    for Consular Affairs

USA FOREIGN AFFAIRS MINISTRY
WASHINGTON D.C.
USA

SUREN ▨▨▨▨▨▨
(Veteran of world War II)
Artist-pedagogue
Republic of ARMENIA
Yerevan 375014

My request is to find my grandchildren and return them
to their Country:
    DAVID ▨▨▨▨▨▨ born in 1985
    DIANA ▨▨▨▨▨▨ born in 1989

My daughter-in-law SVETLANA ▨▨▨▨▨ stealthily went away
from her home and Country in June 1996, taking her children with
her. Secretly from her husband she had received an entrance visa
to the USA from someone completely unknown to her. The children
studied at school Nº782 in Moscow, where my son's family had move
ed for the last years.

Soon it will be a year that we have no news from them. Their
father is our only son. He is a scholar, honest, devoted family
man.

The only data about them we've got are; code 1405-tel.5211010
and 8304340. Recently we've found out that the locality is Okla-
homa City. I wrote to the authorities of the city about four
months ago'but received no answer.

I've applied to the USA Embassy in Armenia, but no answer has
come.

Now this is my last hope, please help me find my grandchildren.

Thank you ever so much.

Gratefully yours

18 Sept. 1997   Suren ▨▨▨▨▨

To the Governing Body of the social
maintenance of the USA

From Souren ▓▓▓▓ 56
address: ▓▓▓▓▓▓▓ compart
ment ▓▓▓▓▓▓ 375014 Armenia
71

Dear leaders of Social maintenance of the USA.
I apply for a help to you to find my grandchilderen.
On October 10th 1996, my son's wife Svetlana ▓▓▓▓
(▓▓▓▓), father's name is Henrik ▓▓▓▓, has left for
the USA taking with her the childern as well
without her husband's permission.
New they are in USA and we don't know in what
city they are living now. I know only that they
have left for the USA from Moscow. My son's wife's
parents live here in yerevan, in Armenia by the
following address: ▓▓▓▓▓▓▓▓ bb. 1, 23, tl. 56-16-07.
They are the mother in Araksia ▓▓▓▓ (father's
name is ▓▓▓▓), the father is Henrik ▓▓▓▓
(father's name in ▓▓▓▓) They both had visited
them in the summer in 2000 and don't want and
allow us to find them and even to know something
about them.
*My grandson's name is David ▓▓▓▓ (father's
name is ▓▓▓▓). He was born on the first of april
in 1985 in yerevan.
*My granddaughter's name is Diana ▓▓▓▓
(father's name is ▓▓▓▓). She was born on the
17th of may in 1989 in Moscow
I'll be very pleased with you if help me
to find my grandchildern
I hope you'll do it that
Thank you very much.
Souren ▓▓▓▓
12.X.2001.

To President of U.S.A.
B.Clinton

Dear Mr. President

On October 10, 1996, my wife, Svetlana ███████████████,
without my knowledge left for the USA taking along with herself without
my consent our two children who are under age: David ███████████
███████, 12 and Diana ███████████████████, 8. As I found out later
from the American Embassy in Moscow, she got a non-immigration visa
on June 21, 1996, however I was refused to be told whom she got the
invitation from. Also, in the embassy they advised me to hire a private
investigator in the USA for locating the whereabouts of my children.
Later was revealed quite a member of tricks and forgeries that my wife
undertook when leaving for the USA.

Mr. President, I immensely respect your country, the freedom-loving
and democratic aspirations of the United States are very dear to me, but
allowing my wife to stay in America in breach of the laws, concealing
her whereabouts, the agencies in change become participators in her
venture thereby encouraging transgression of the law. From the height of
the presidential seat the problem that makes me turn namely to you may
seen an insignificant one, but for me being separated from my beloved
children, being unawares of even their whereabouts is a tragedy beyond
compare. And if at present I don't have the means to hire private
investigators in the US, does it mean that I have to be deprived of seeing
my children?

Sending you this letter I hope, I do want to hope, to get your
assistance.

Respectfully,

███████████

███████████,
Erevan 375014, Armenia

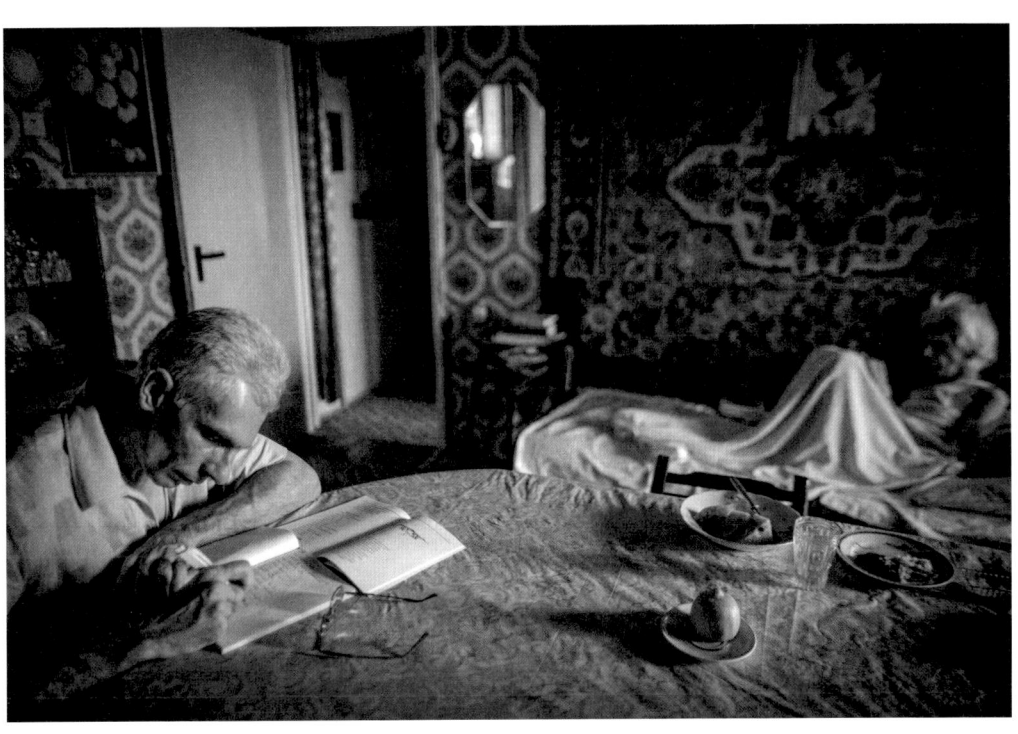

I listen to him speak about the past.
My parents met in university.
My mother had just turned 21.
This is the first time I am seeing pictures of them together.
They look so happy, so in love.
All I ever heard was her anger:
"He made his decisions, and we're making ours."

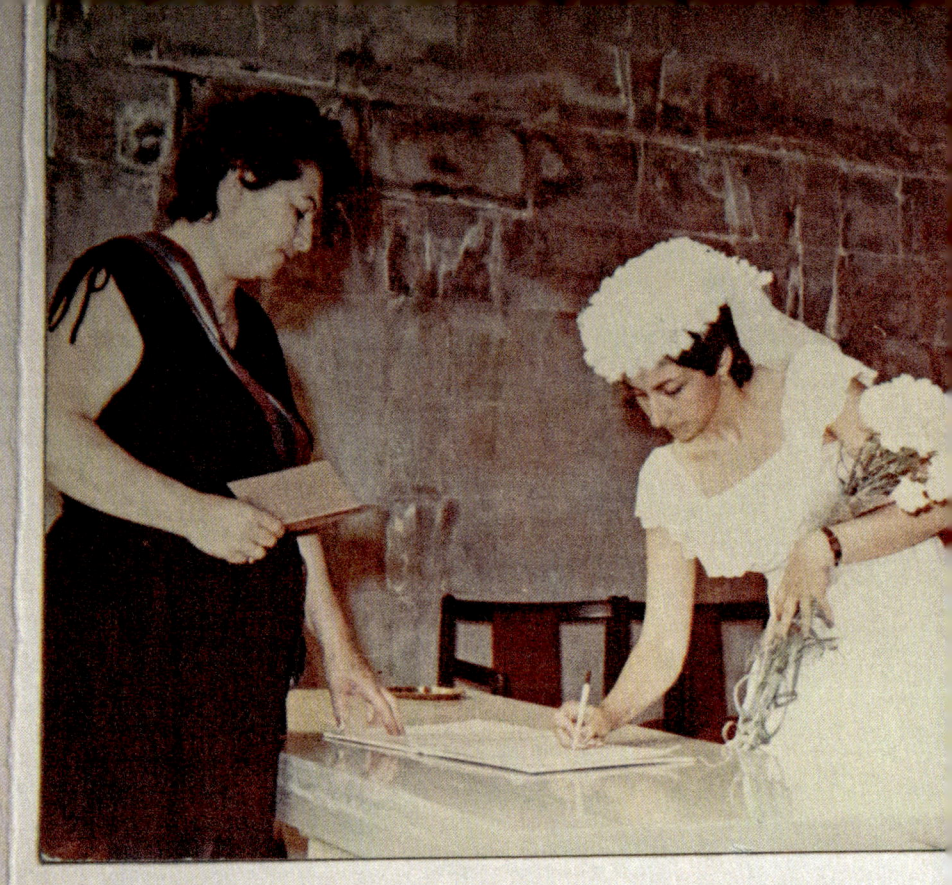

3   Июля.

1984 года

3 июля 1984 год

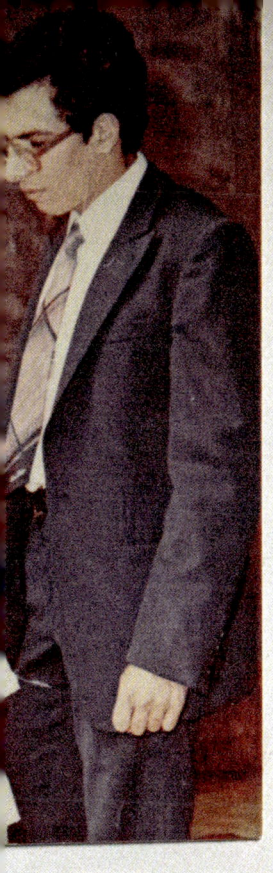

Дворец
бракосочетания

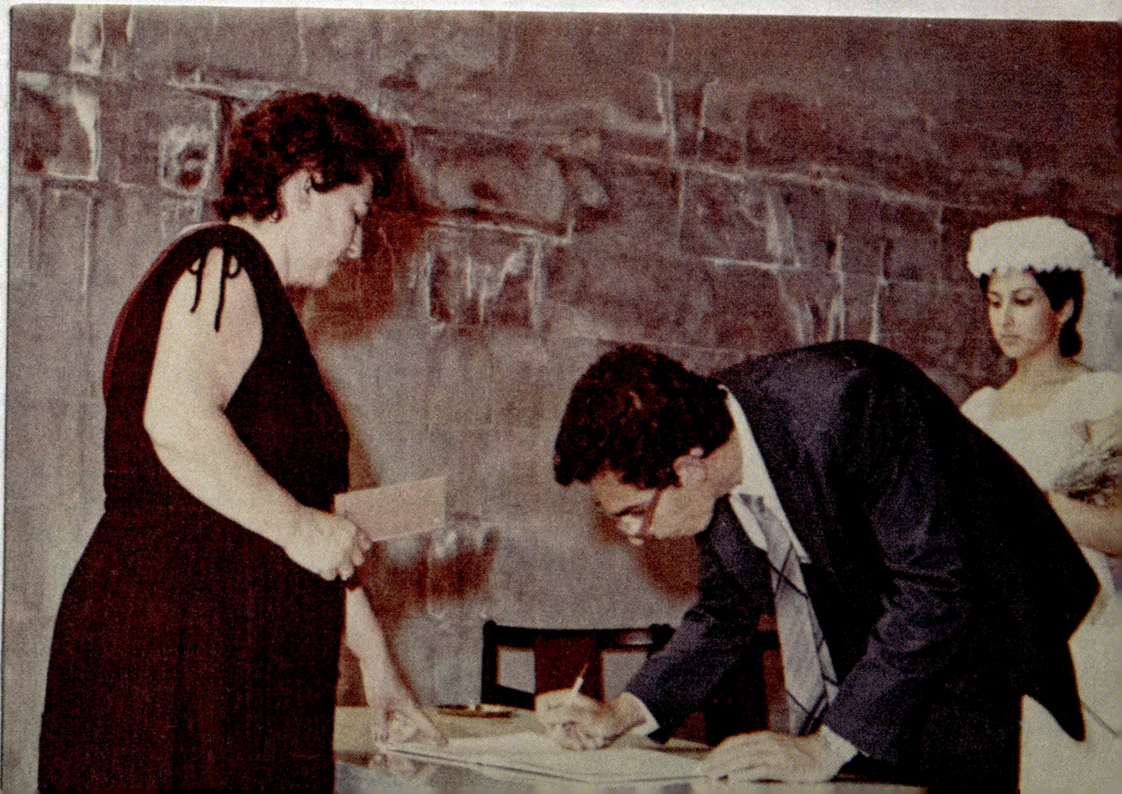

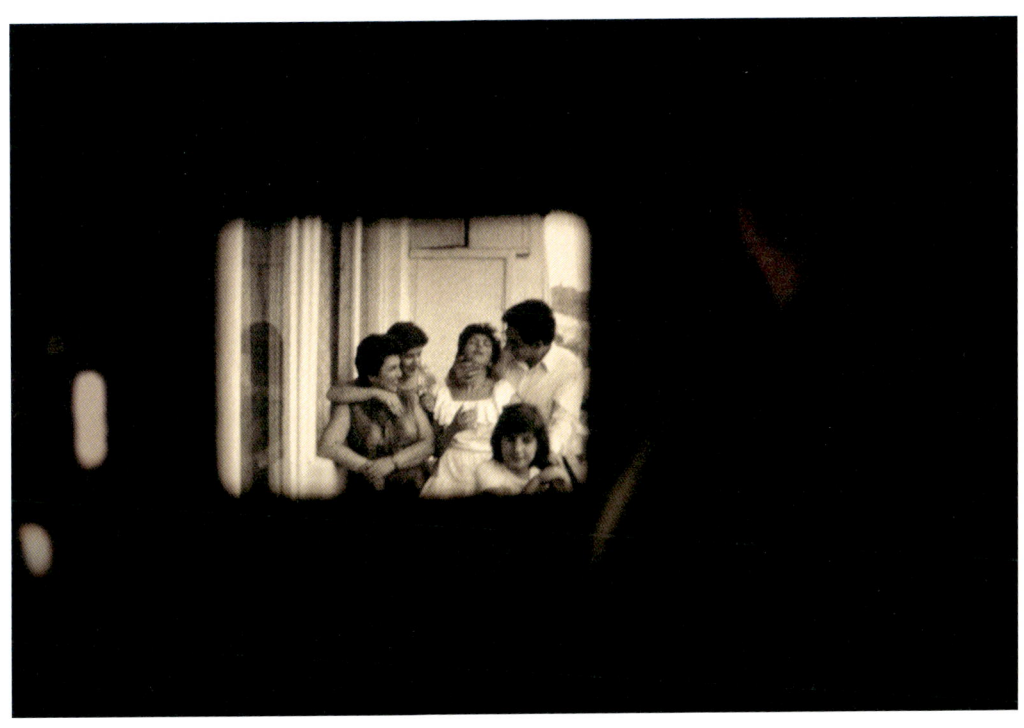

He loads a cassette into a tape player.
I hear my younger voice.
He asked if I knew what divorce was.
"Yes," I said.
"Is divorce a good thing?" he asked.
I cried and told him I didn't know.
"Do you want your mom and dad to get divorced?"
I cried more.
"I don't."

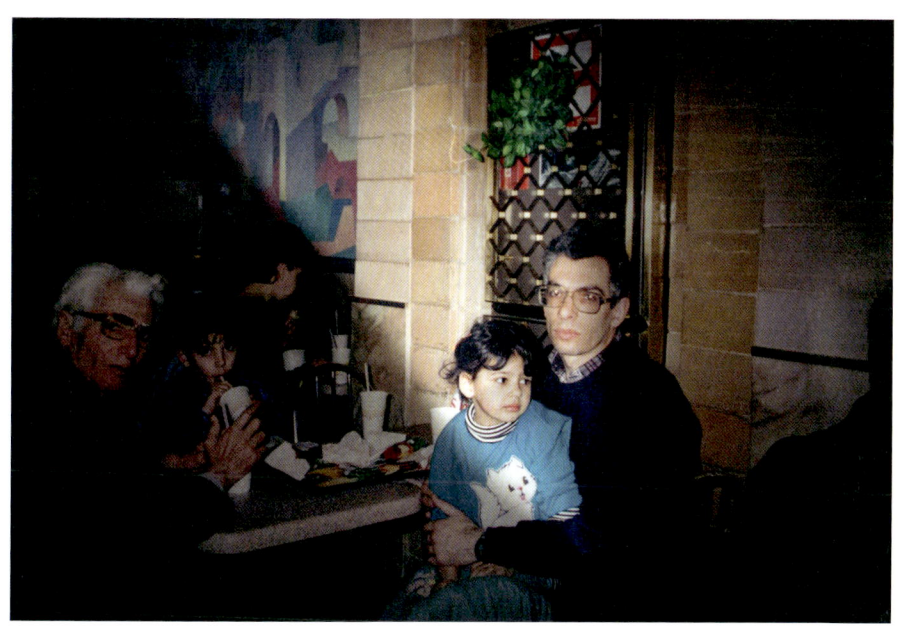

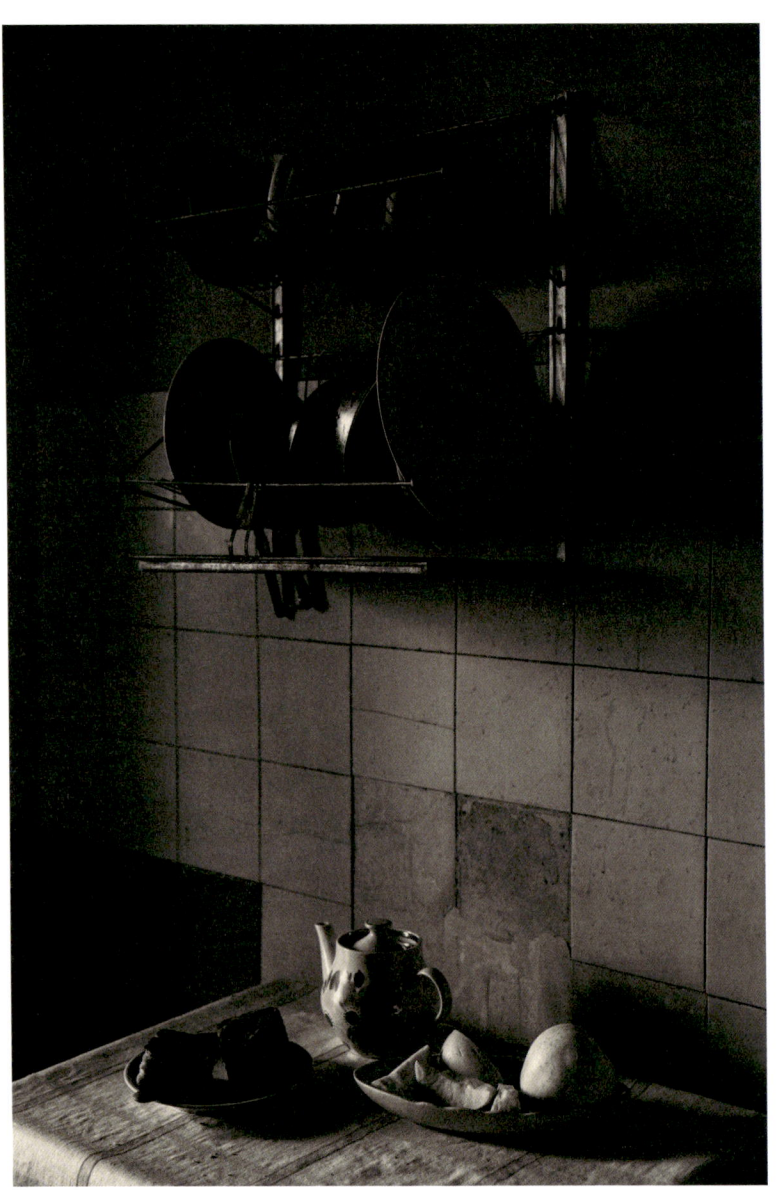

The recording takes me back to our family apartment in Moscow.

In the kitchen,
my parents yelling,
my brother crying,
my father leaving.

Sometimes he would disappear for weeks or months at a time.

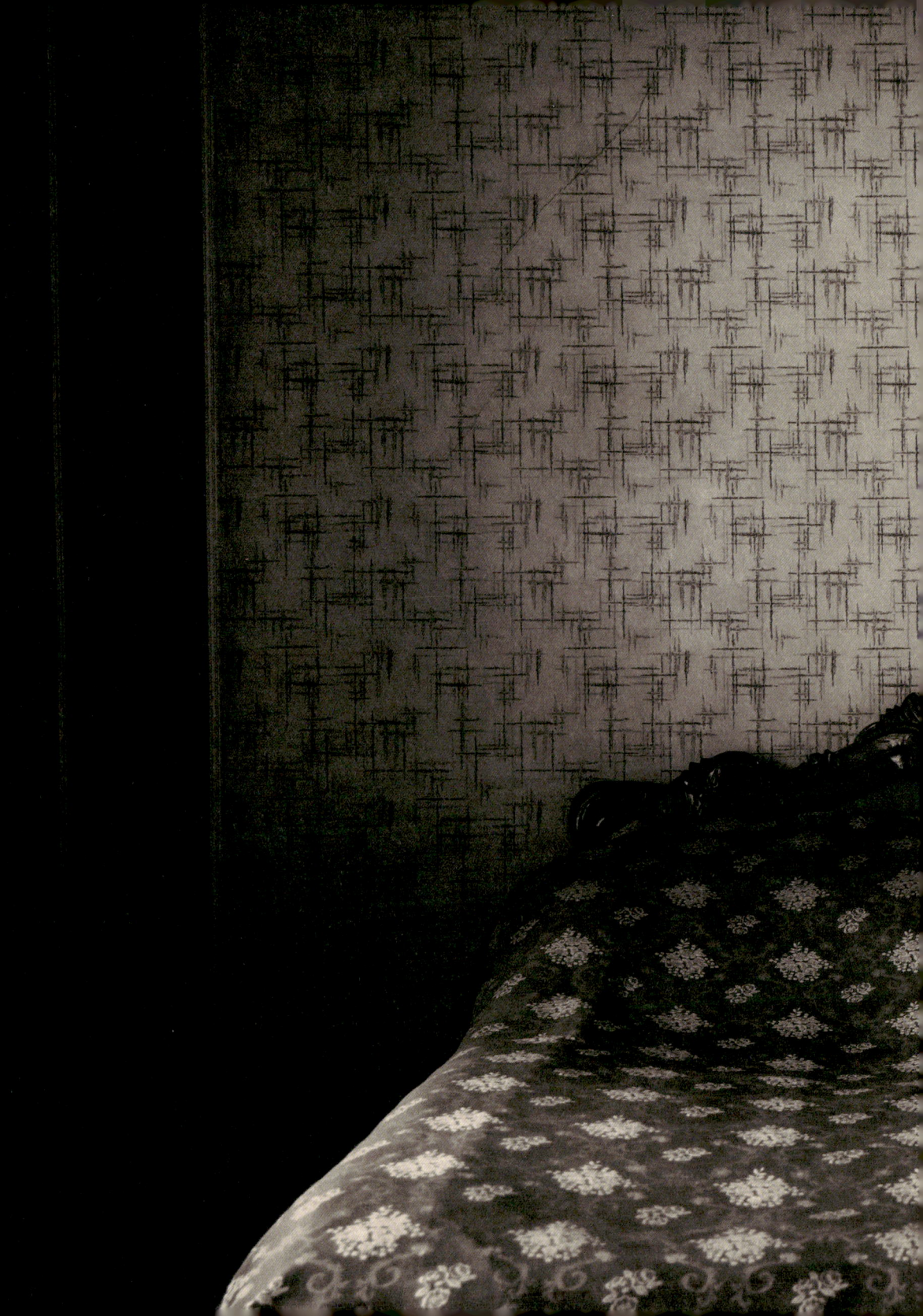

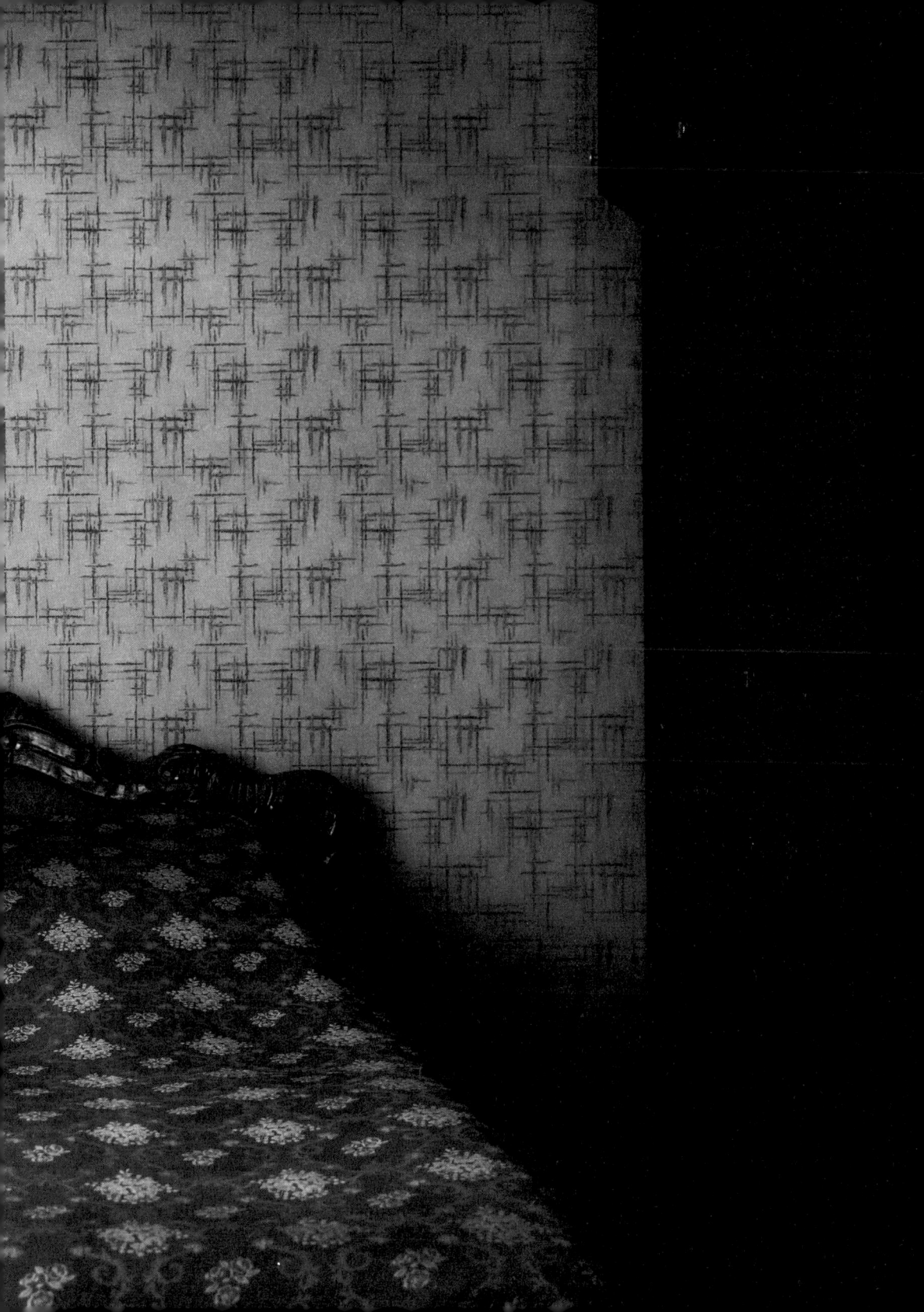

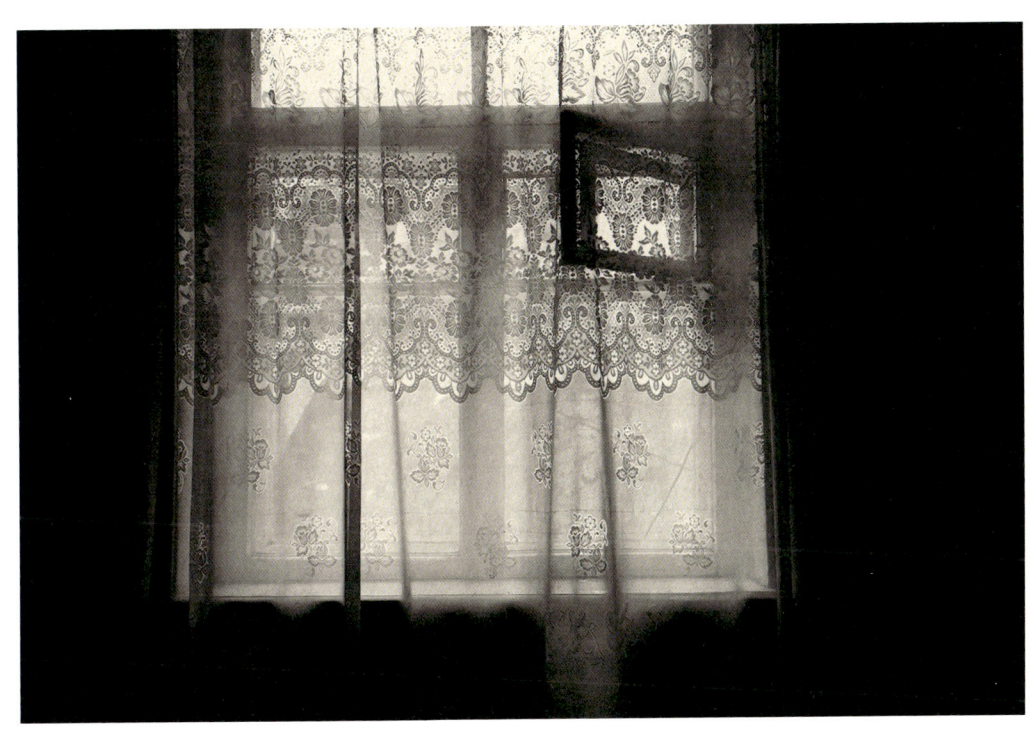

He asks me to stay with him.
We spend mornings together,
my father sitting across the kitchen table.

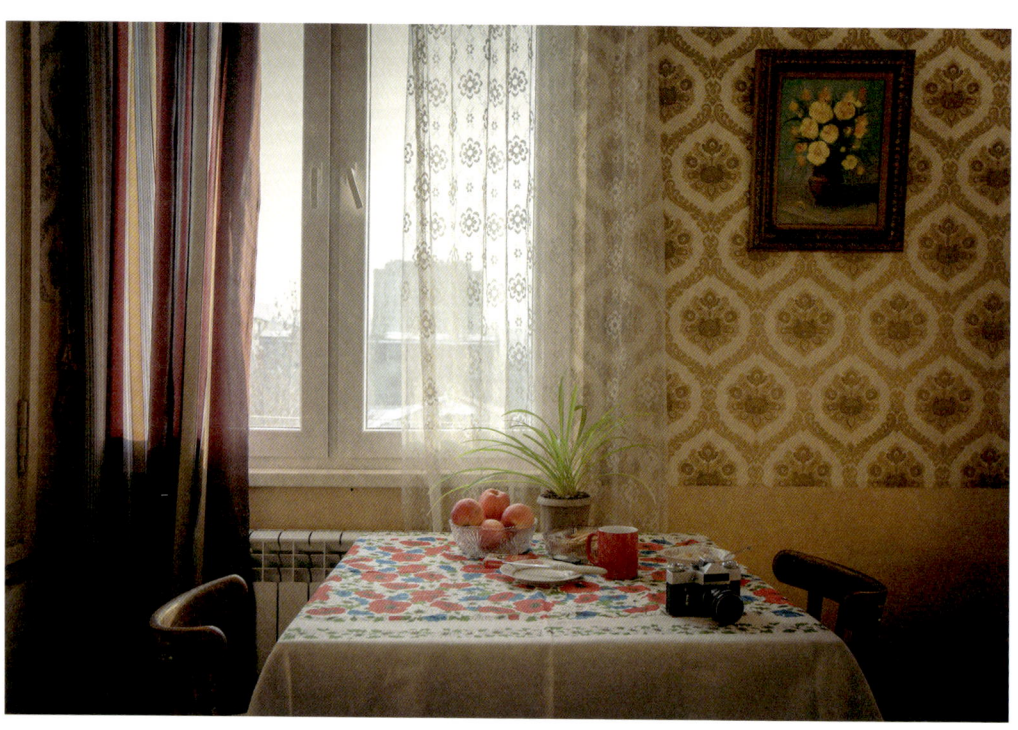

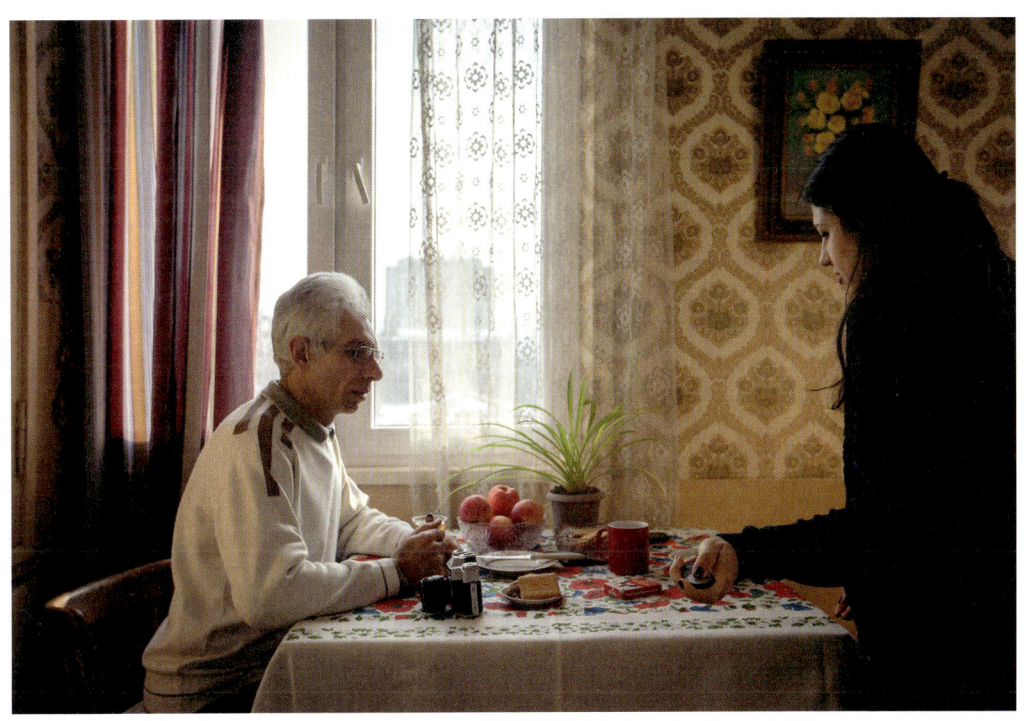

Monday, 10:27 a.m.

I ask you to make us breakfast.
You prepare an omelet.
We eat it out of a pan, just like you do when you're alone.

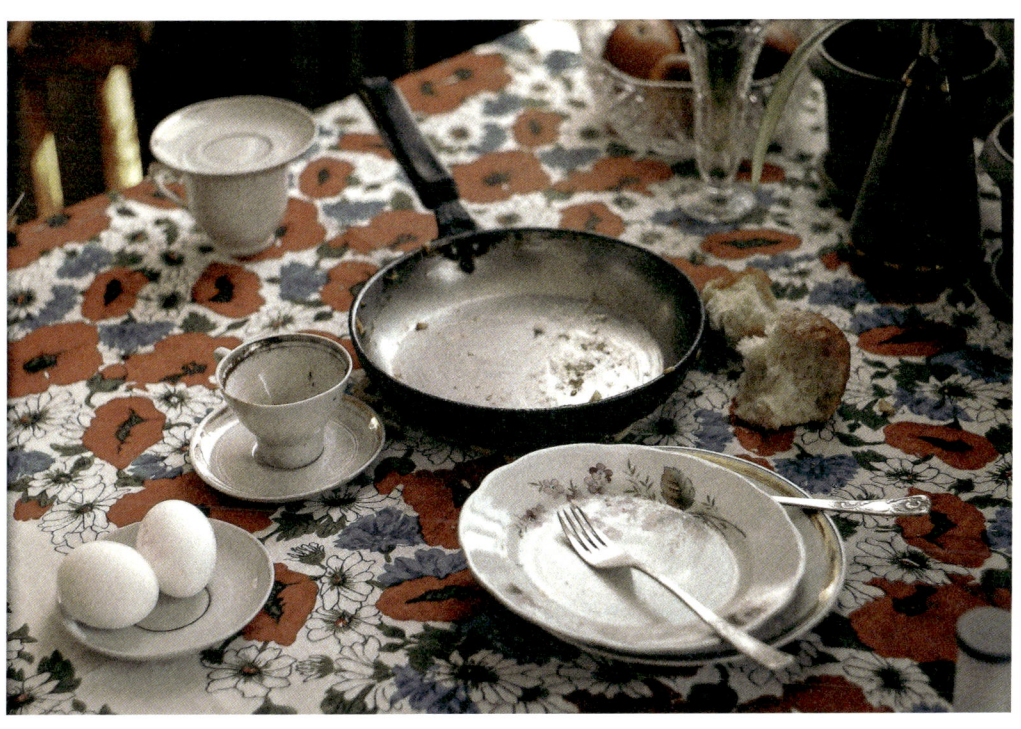

Tuesday, 8:22 a.m.

You ask me about my childhood.
All those years without you.
Where do I start?
The time I danced on stage and looked for you.
My 14th birthday, when I wished for you.
Or my first heartbreak.
I don't know what you want to hear.

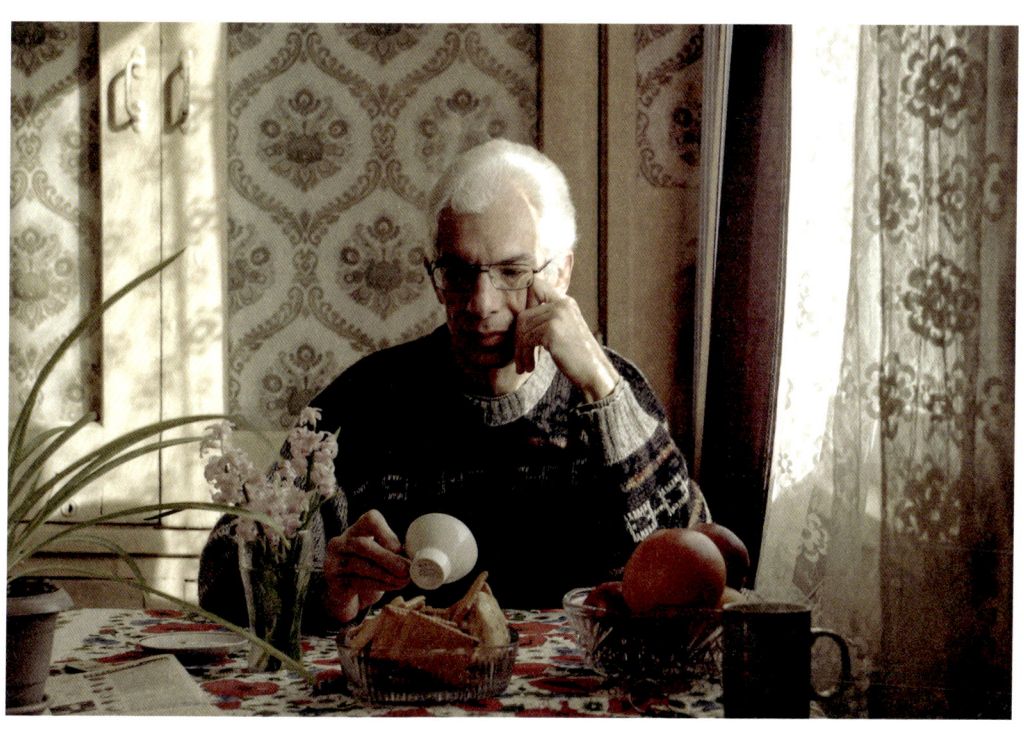

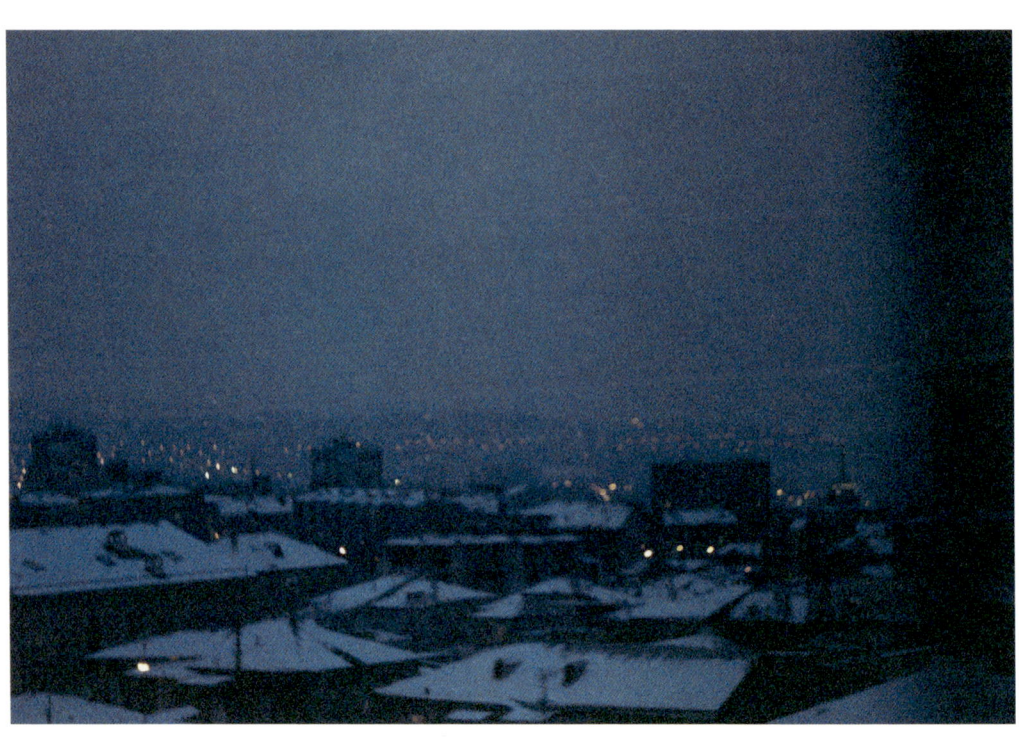

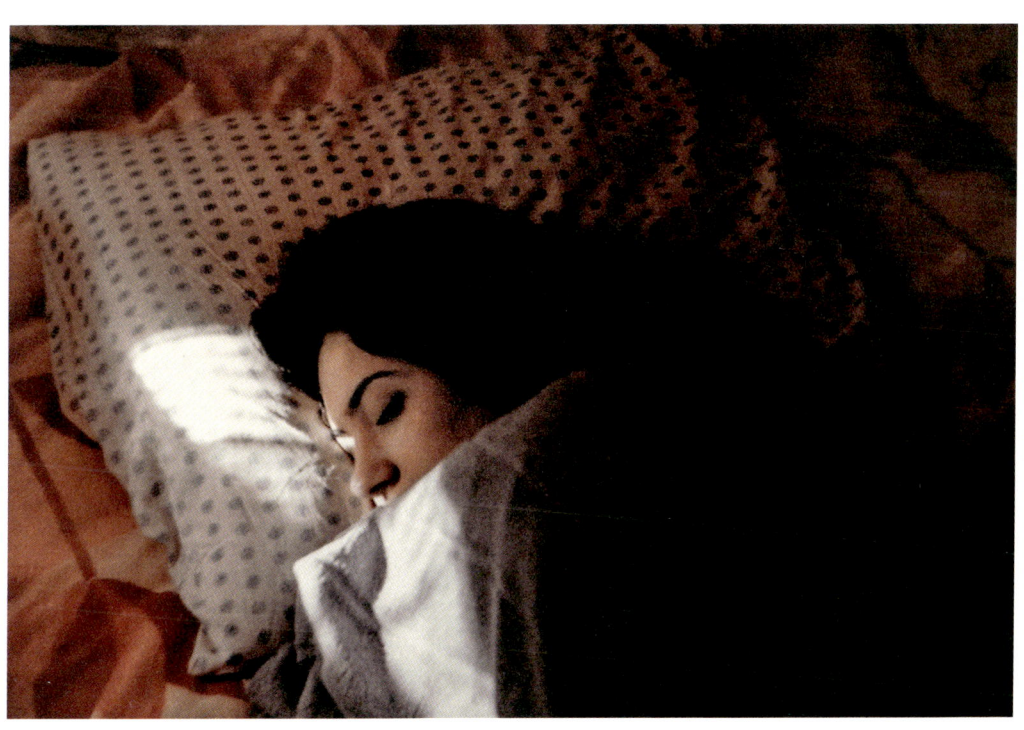

Wednesday, 9:42 a.m.

You're wearing the same sweater you wore on Monday.
I ask you to change.
"I don't have enough sweaters for this project," you say.

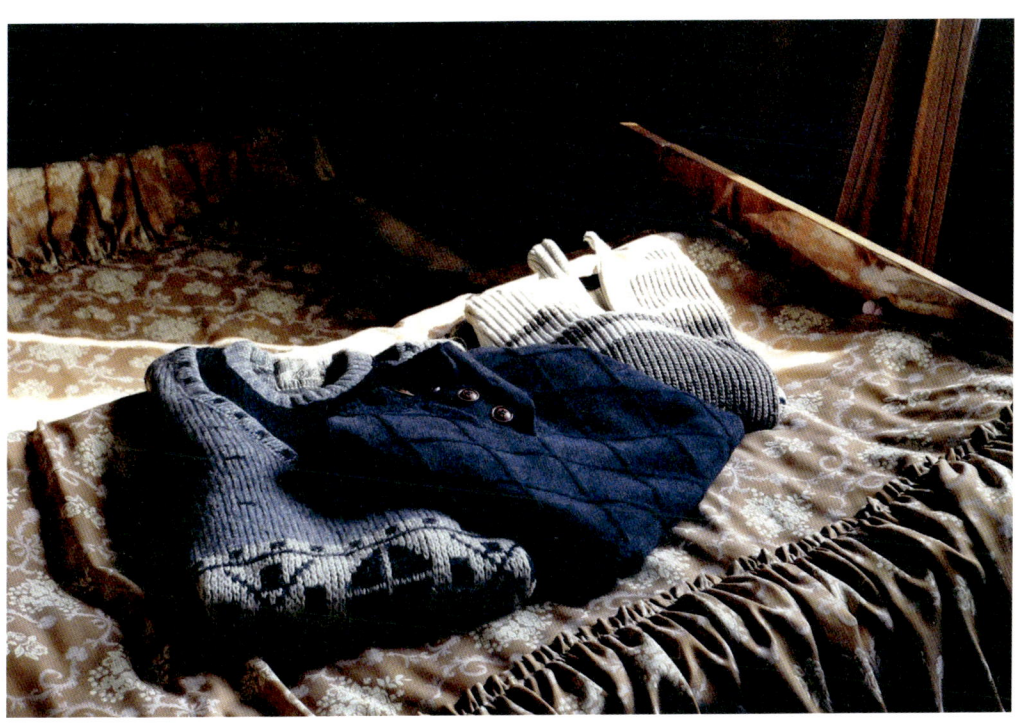

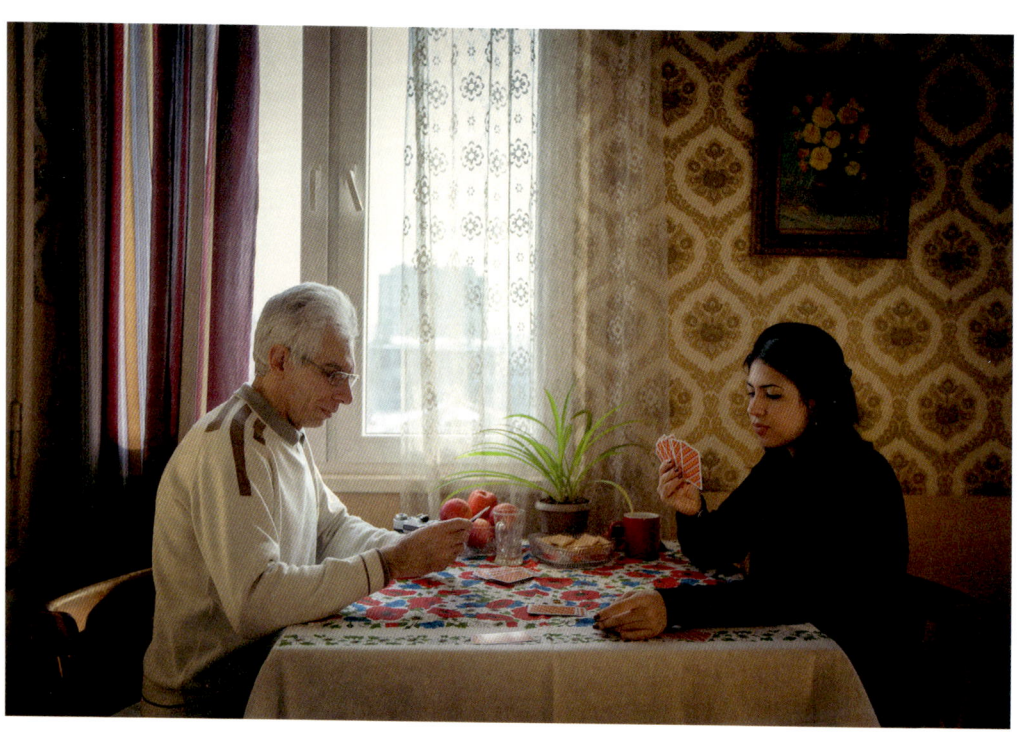

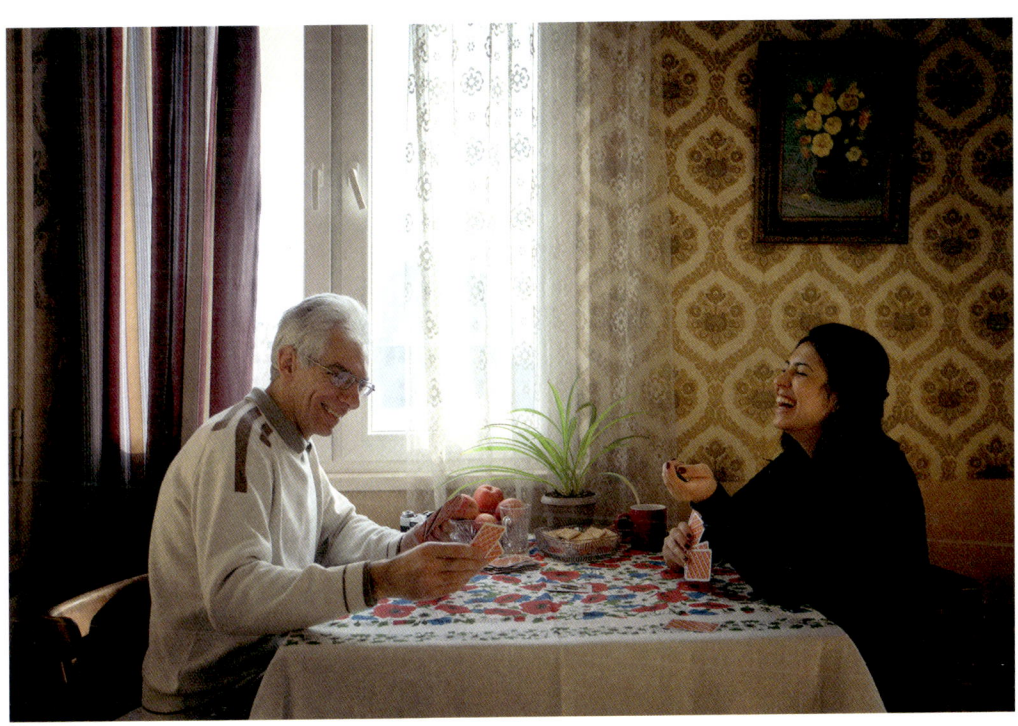

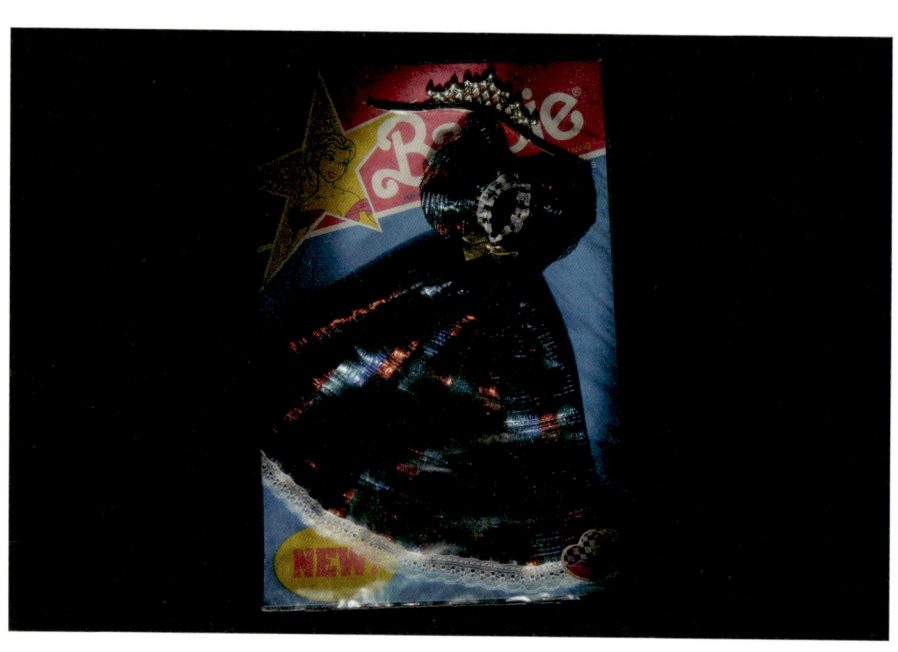

Thursday, 10:02 a.m.

I am learning so much about you.
The little things: you like your coffee dark and sweet.
The big things: you need to create.
Like the Barbie dresses that you made and sold on the street.
It was your first business.
You named it after me.

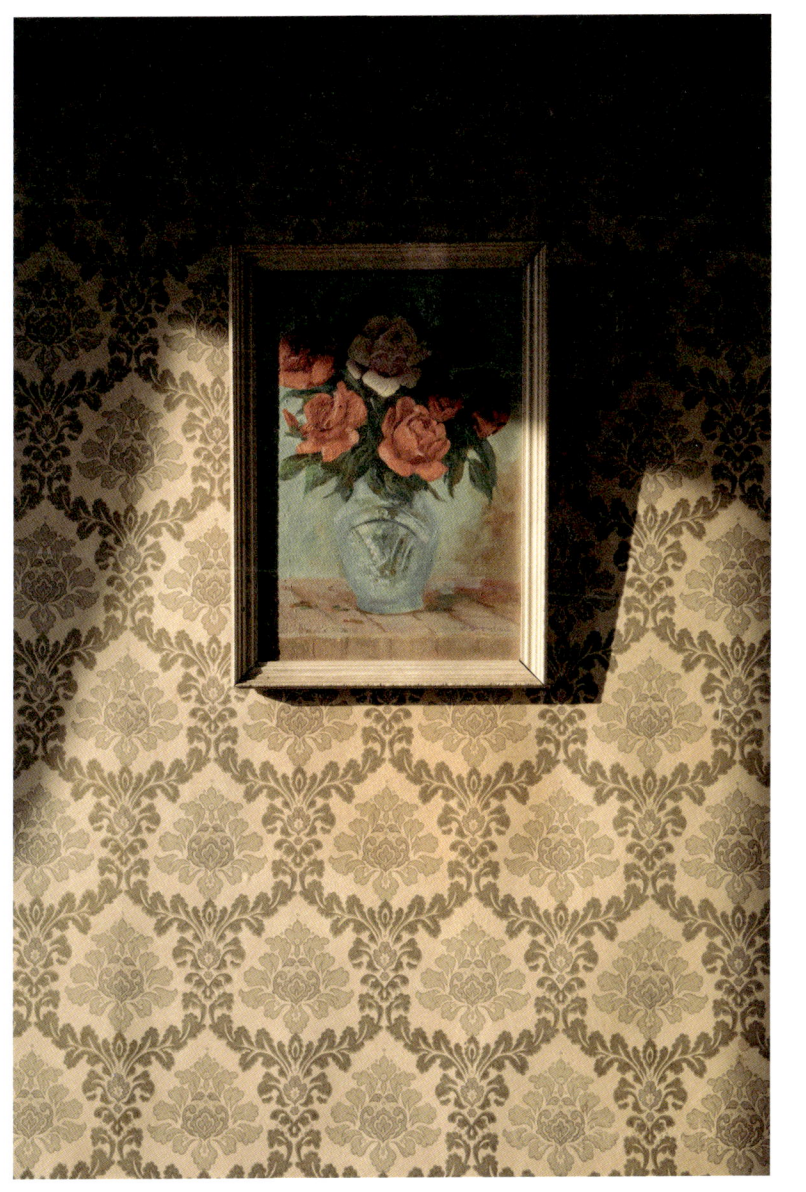

Friday, 10:17 a.m.

I ask you to take a picture of me.
Something you haven't done since I was seven.

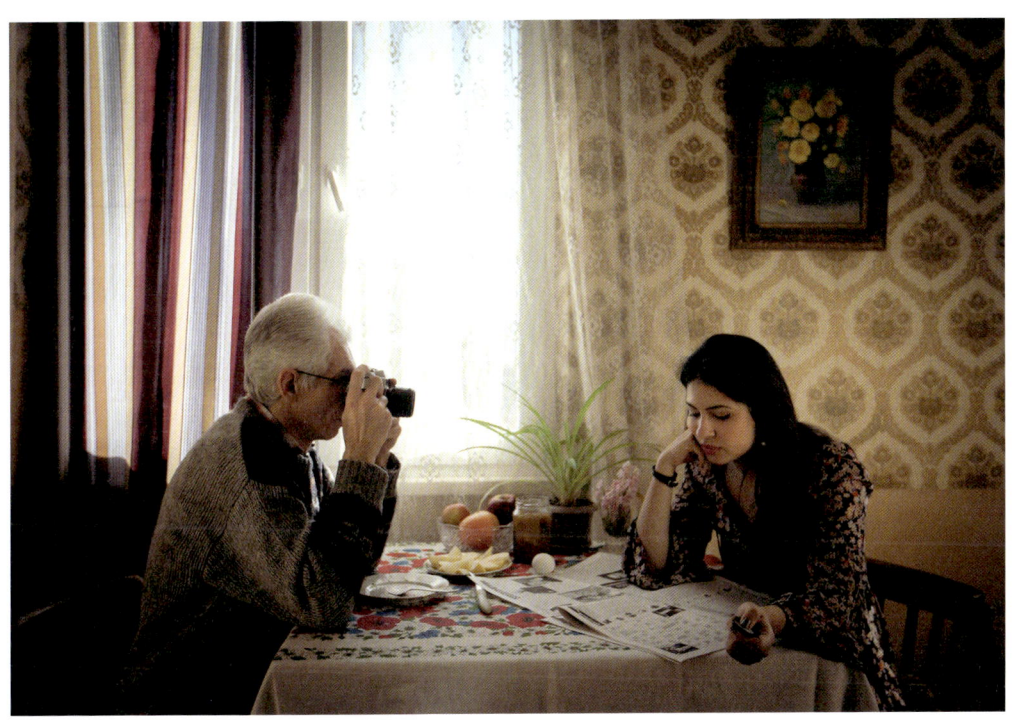

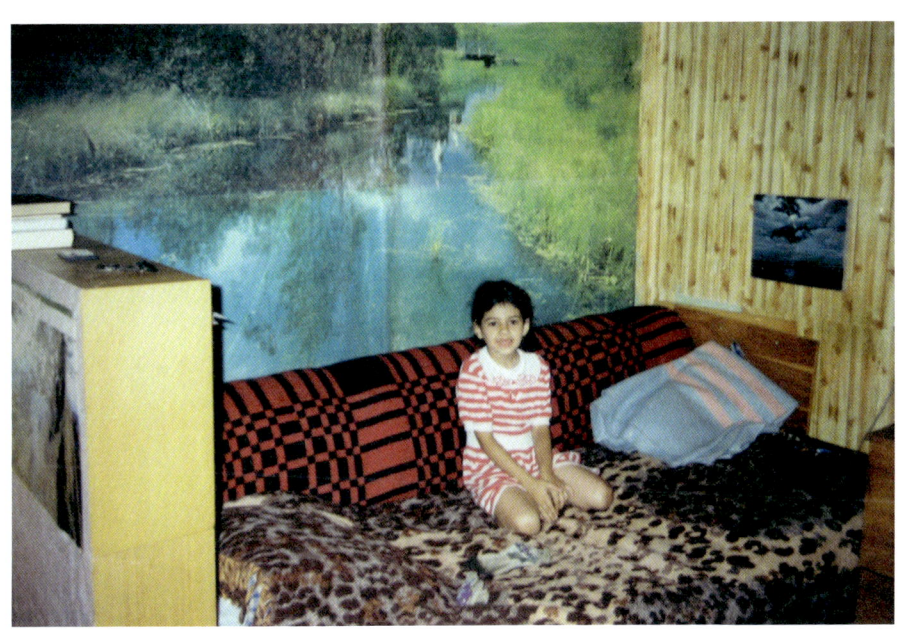

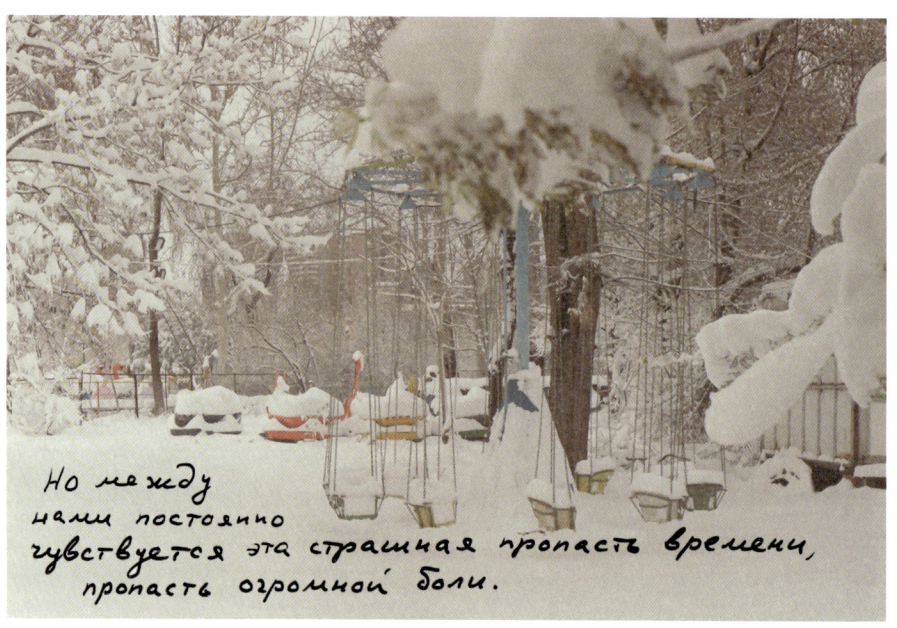

Но между
нами постоянно
чувствуется эта страшная пропасть времени,
пропасть огромной боли.

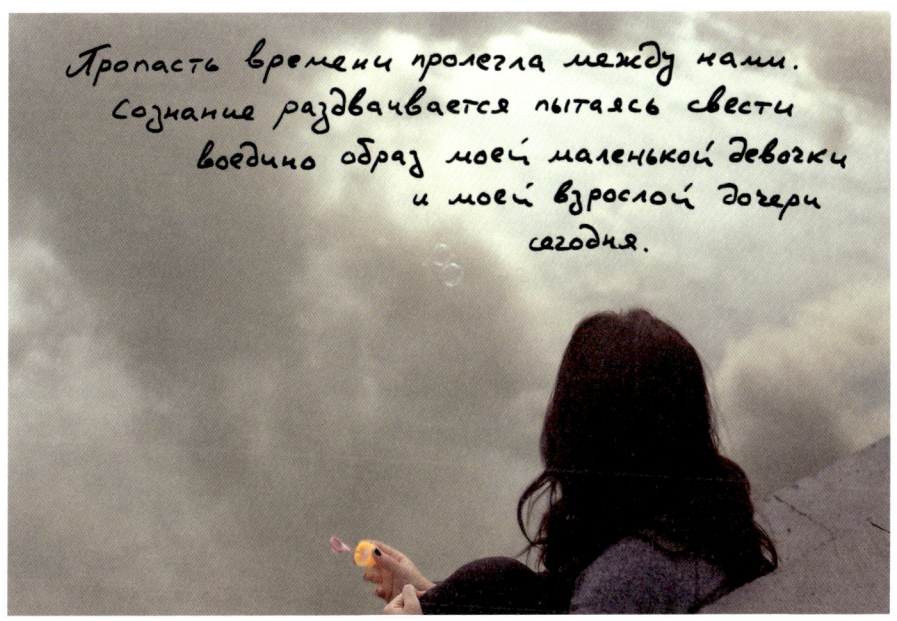

Пропасть времени пролегла между нами.
Сознание раздваивается пытаясь свести
воедино образ моей маленькой девочки
и моей взрослой дочери
сегодня.

On one photograph, you write:

"I am searching for the child in her, the one I used to be close to.
In myself, I am searching for the feelings I once had for her."

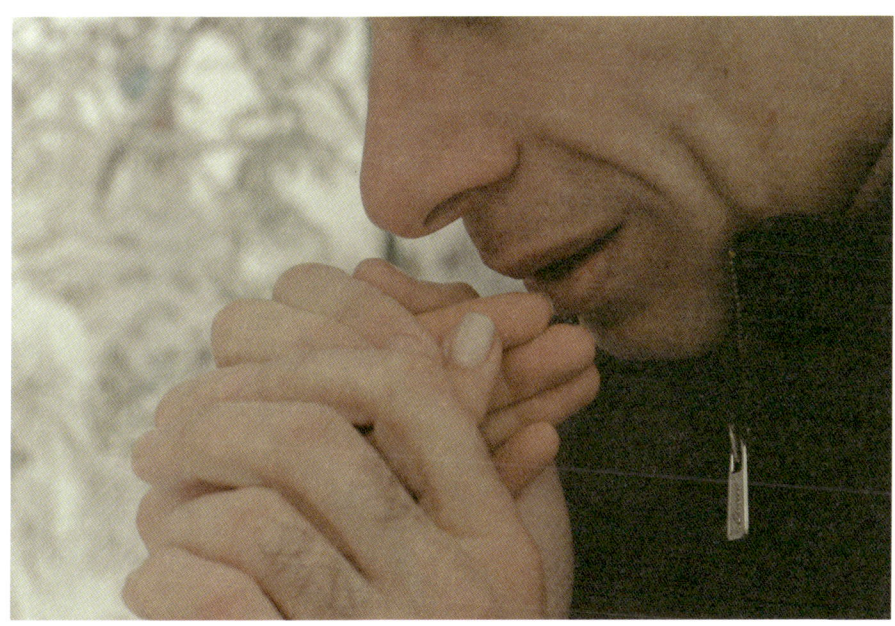

Right after I find him, my father has another child, a little girl.
I should be happy for him, but I am not.
Why does she get to have him, and I don't?

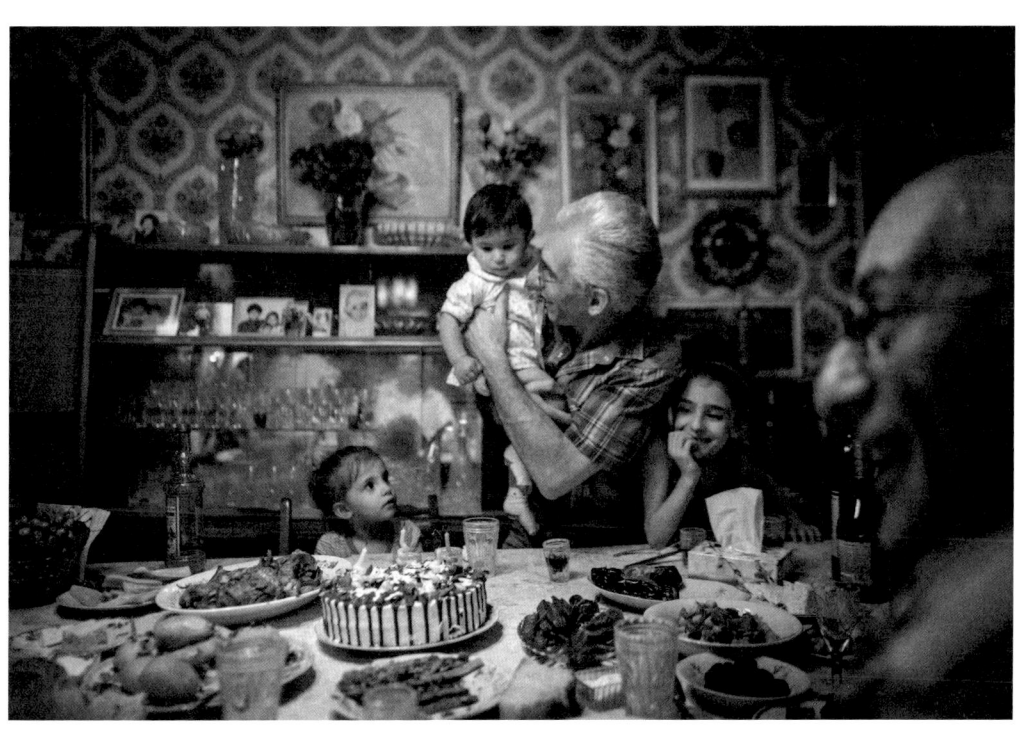

Even now.
He's often not around.
He leaves me alone with my grandfather.

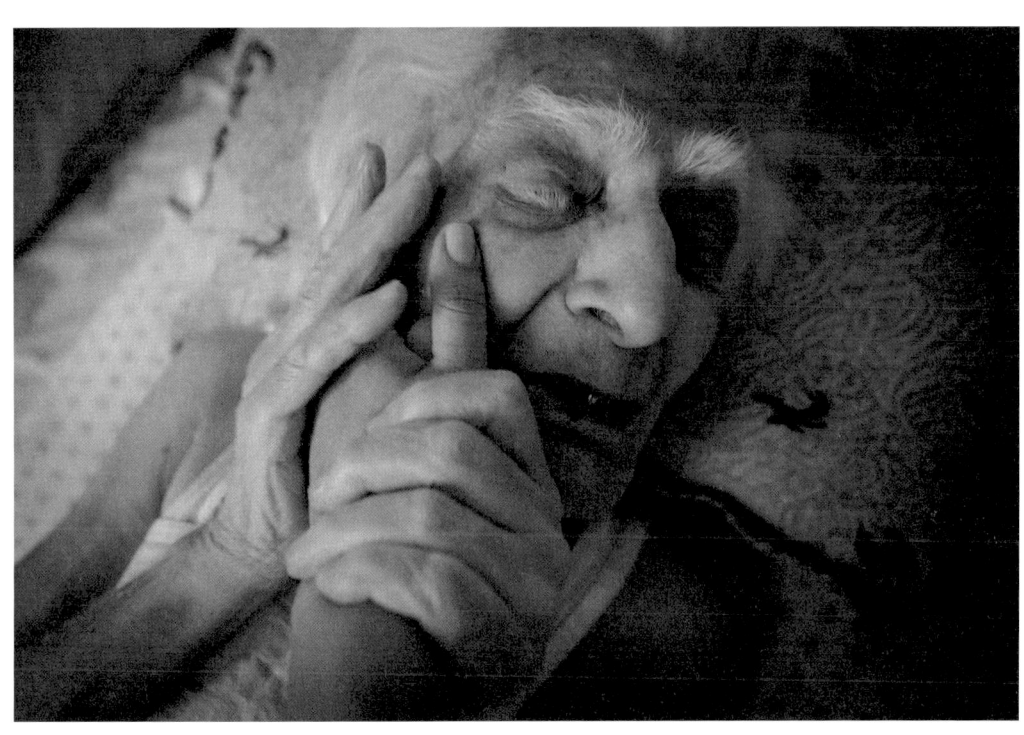

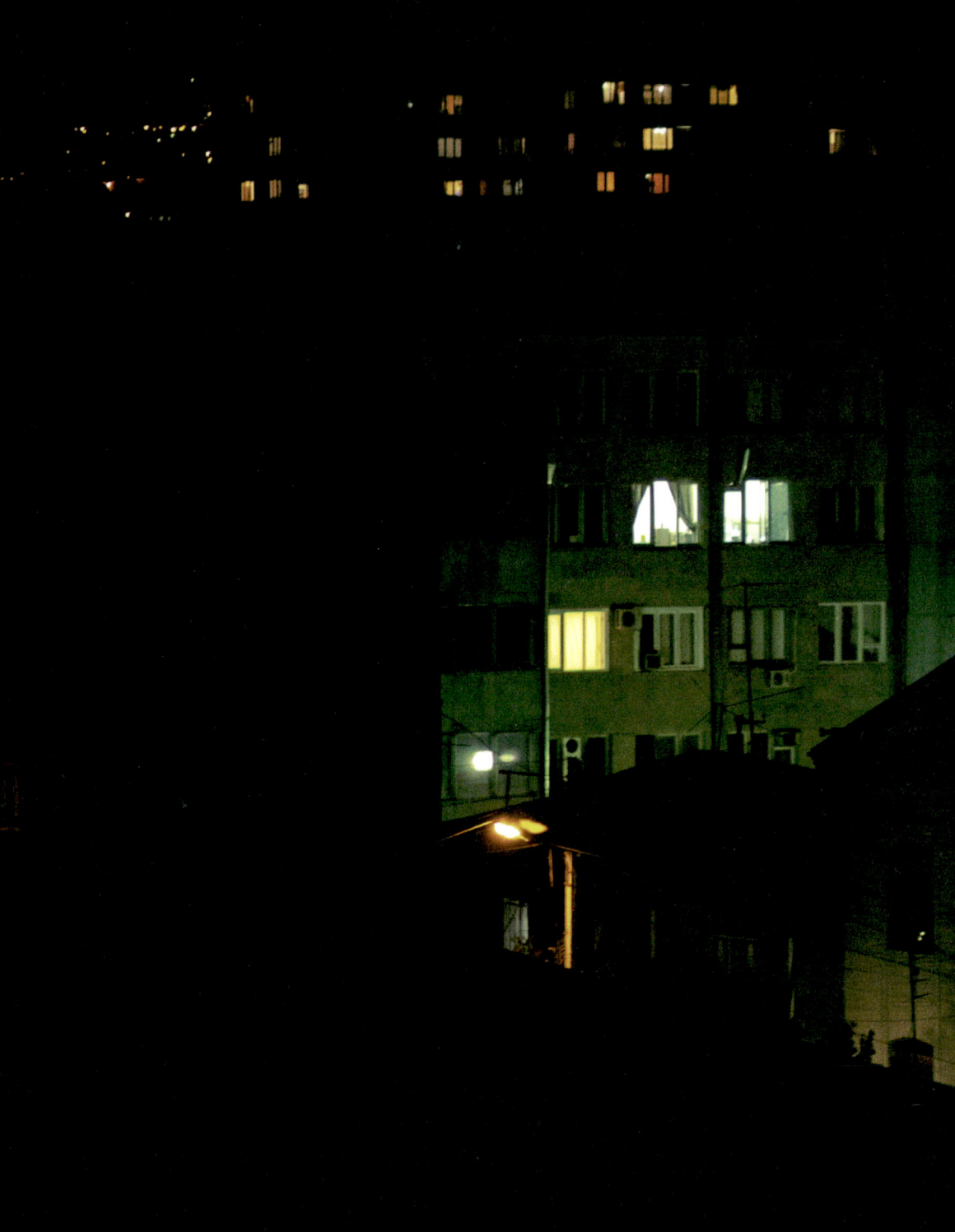

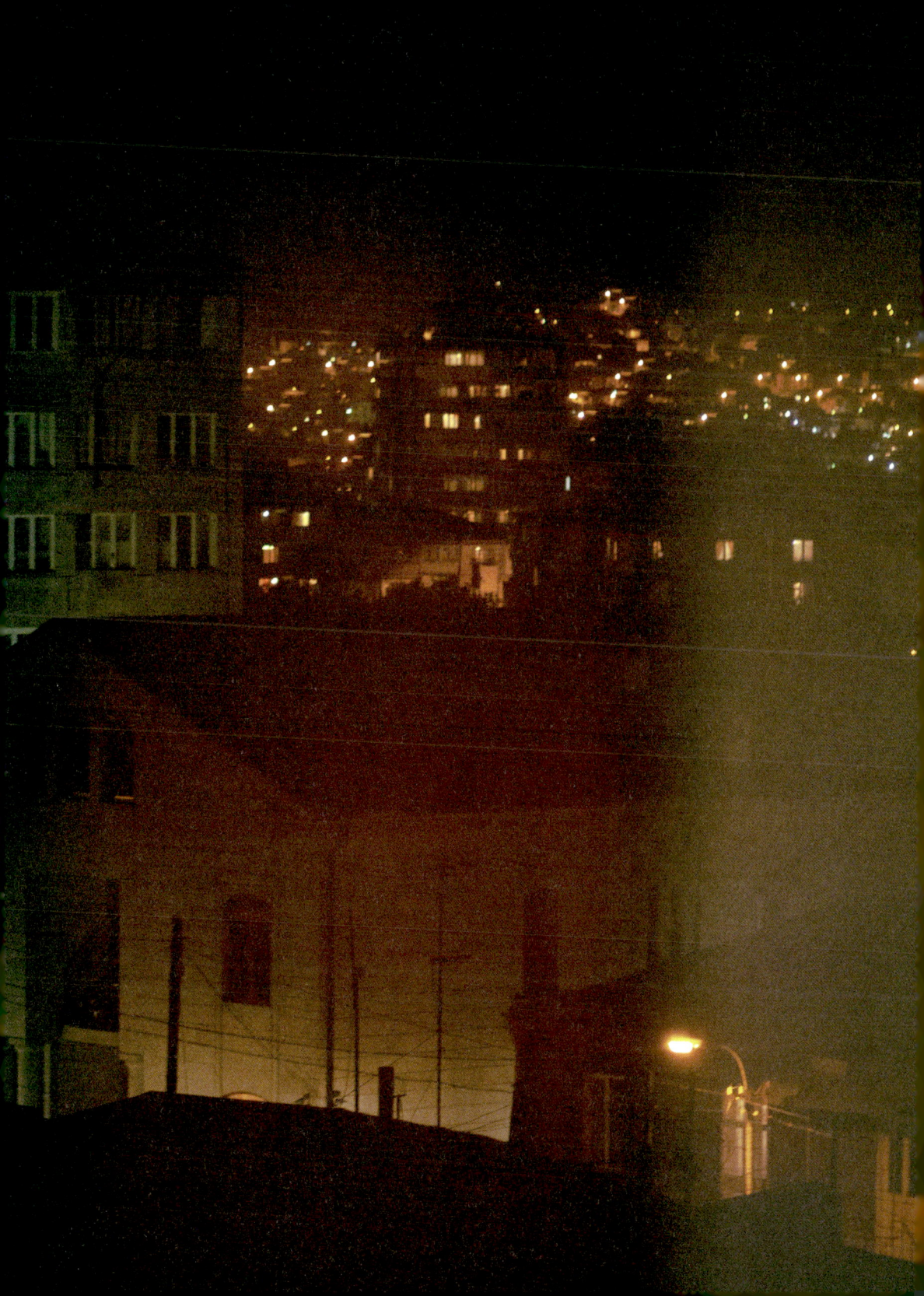

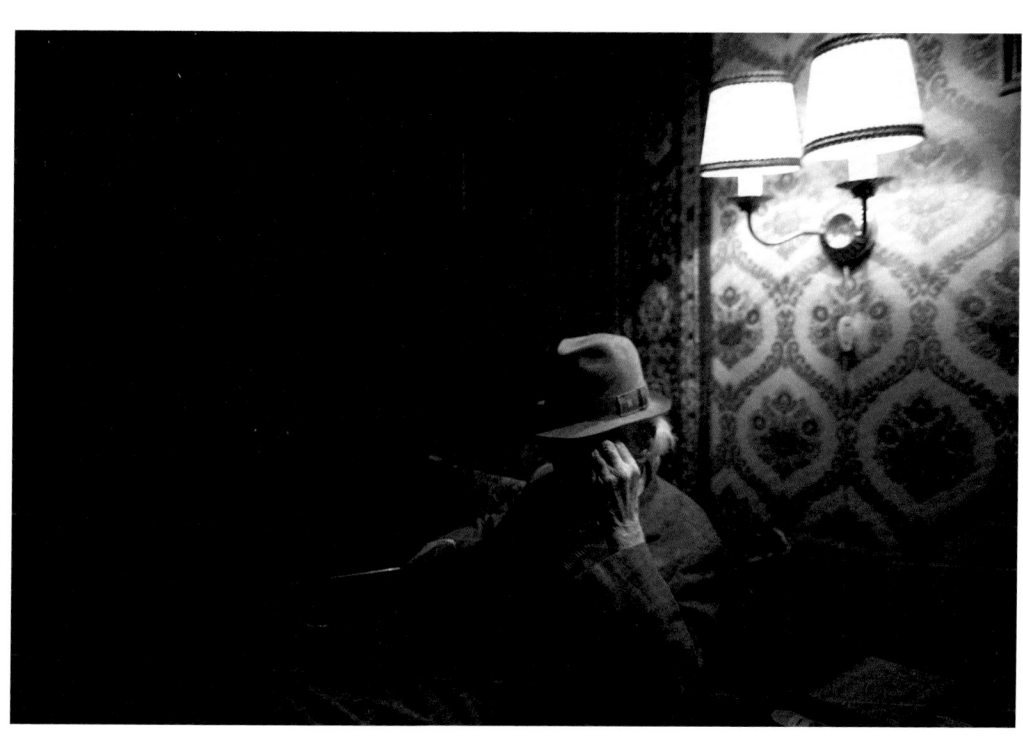

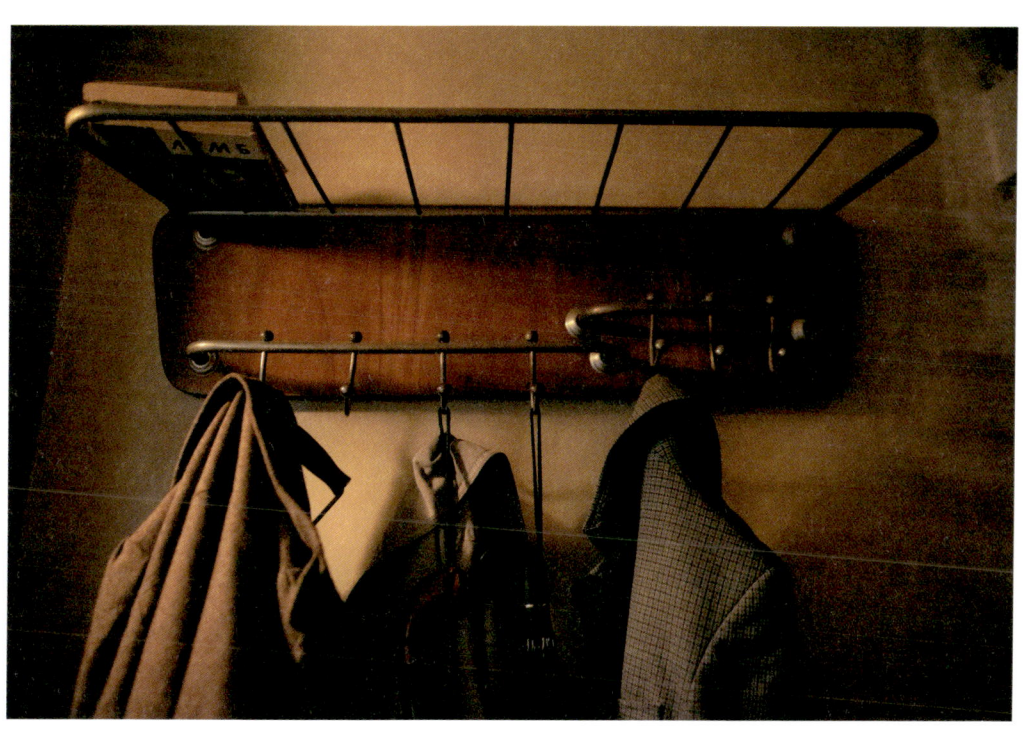

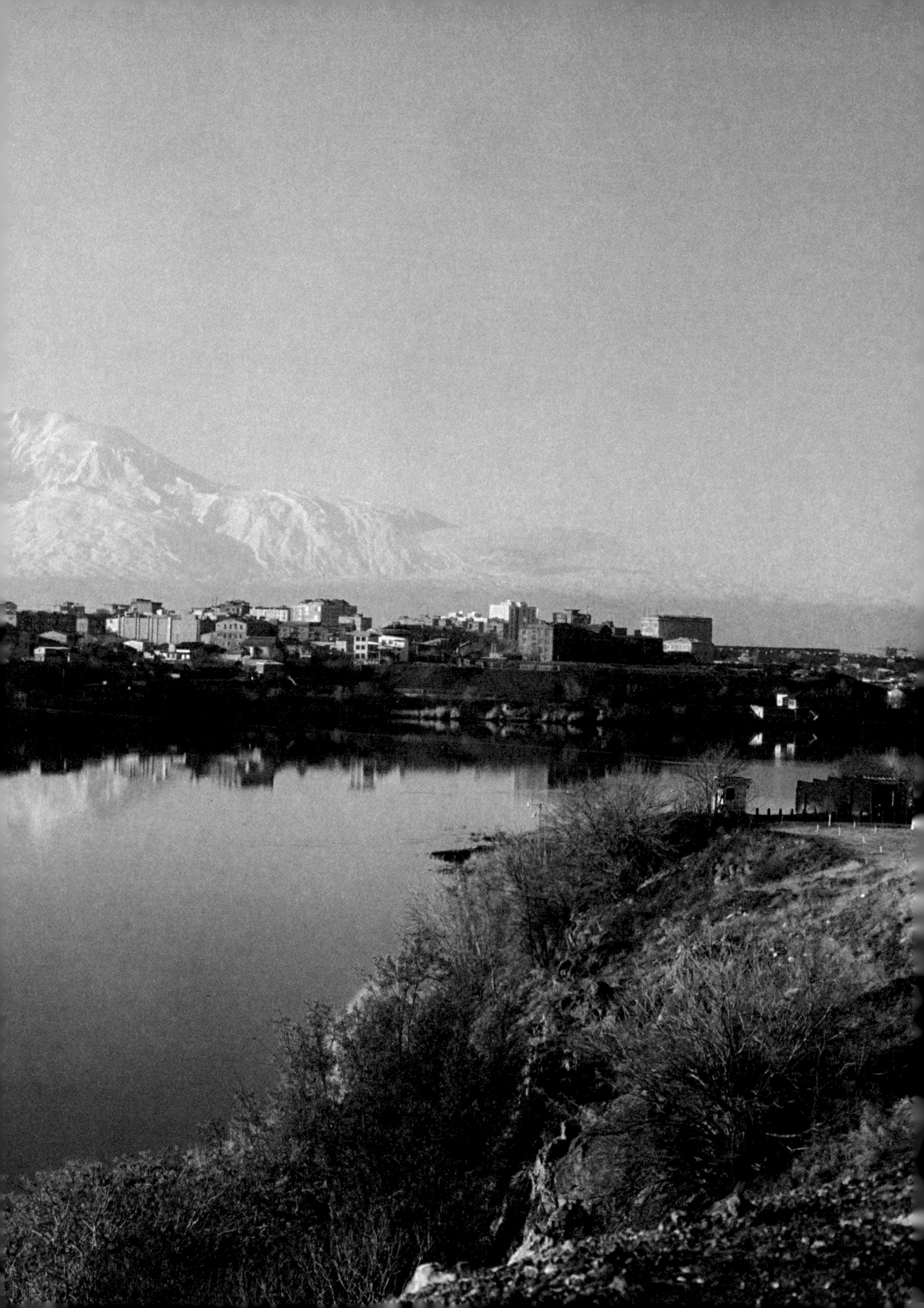

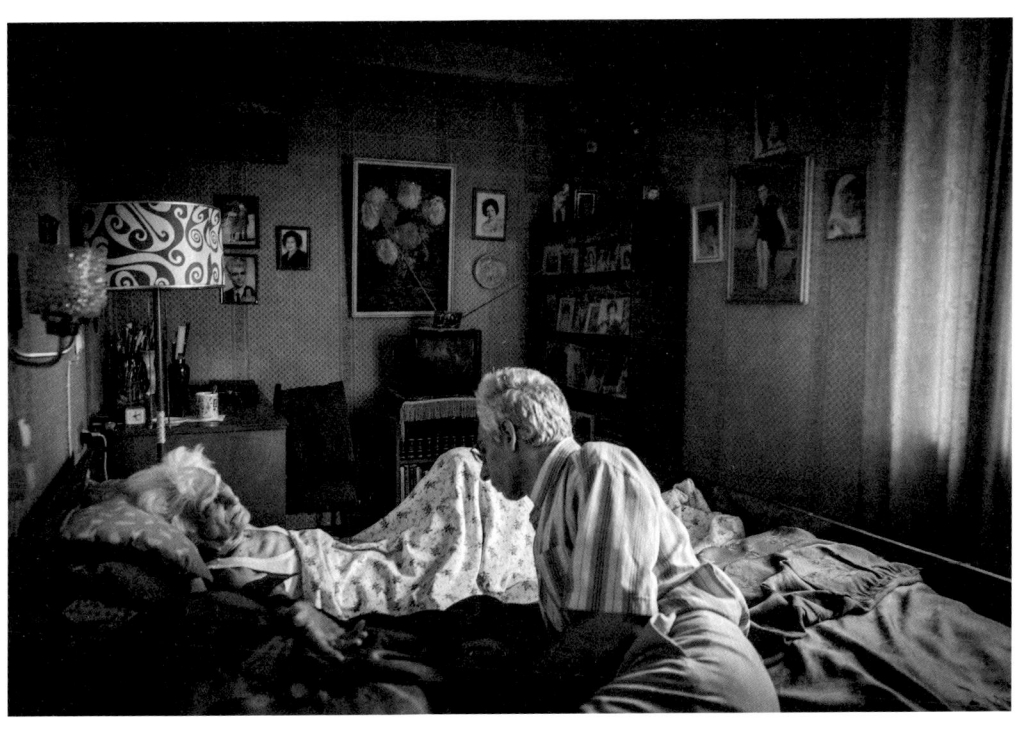

When my father is home,
I often don't know how to behave around him.
Sometimes he watches me brush my hair or reaches to hug me.
I pull away.

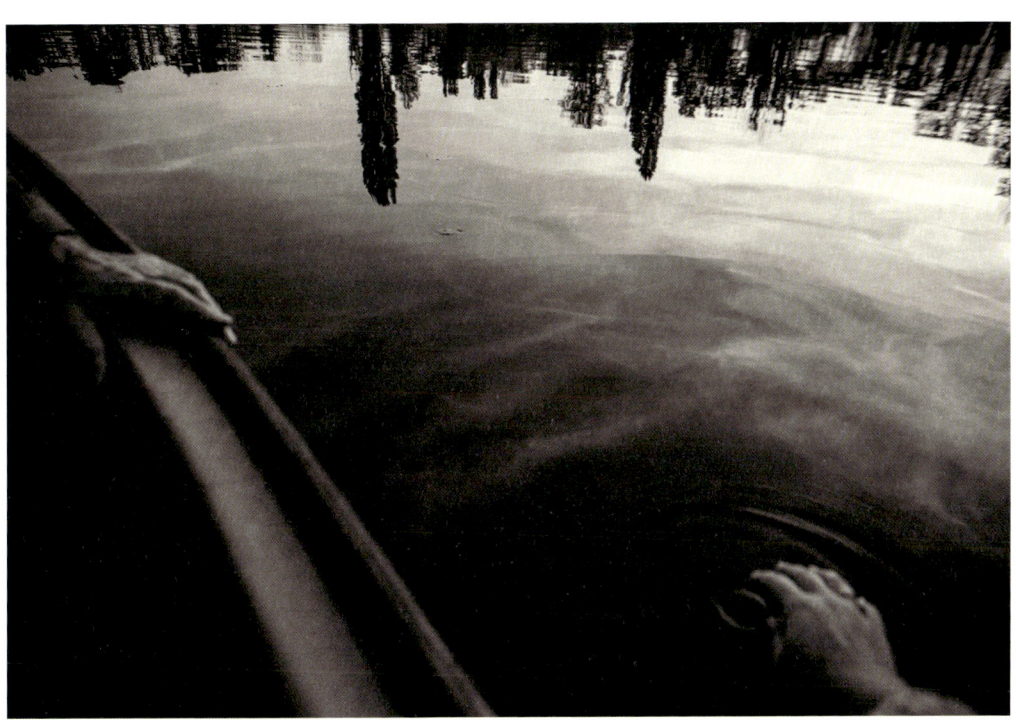

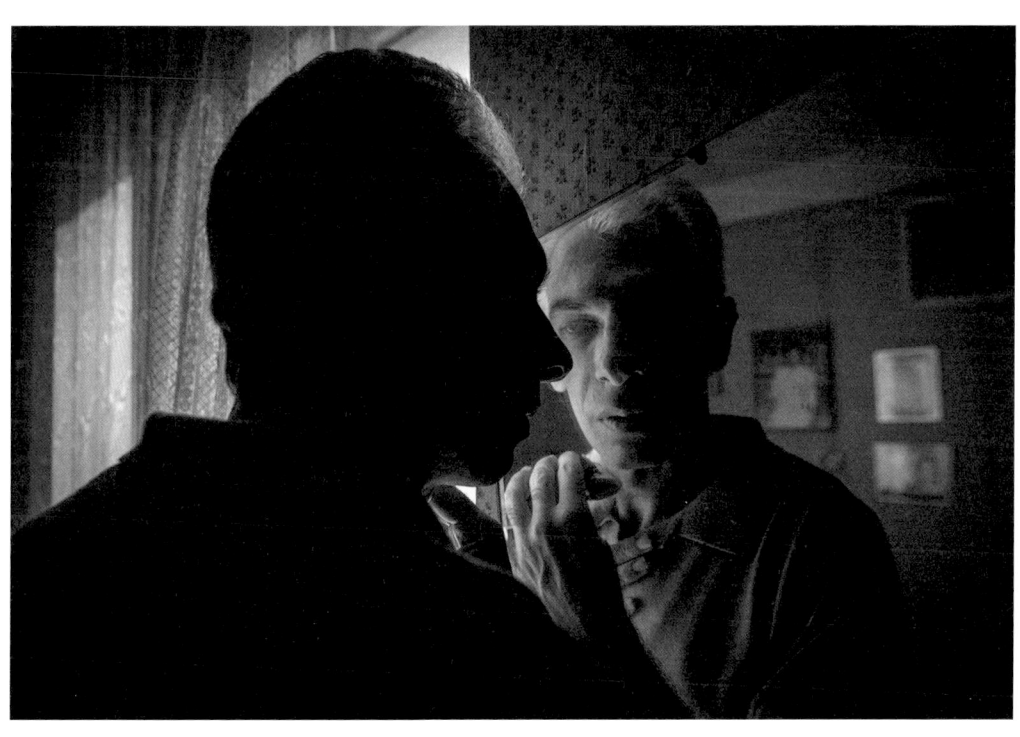

One night, he surprises me with tickets to the symphony.
We dress up together, my father in a button-down and me in a dress.
He sneaks in chocolates; we eat them in the dark.

But then he's gone again.
To his new life.

"It's not the best time," he says.

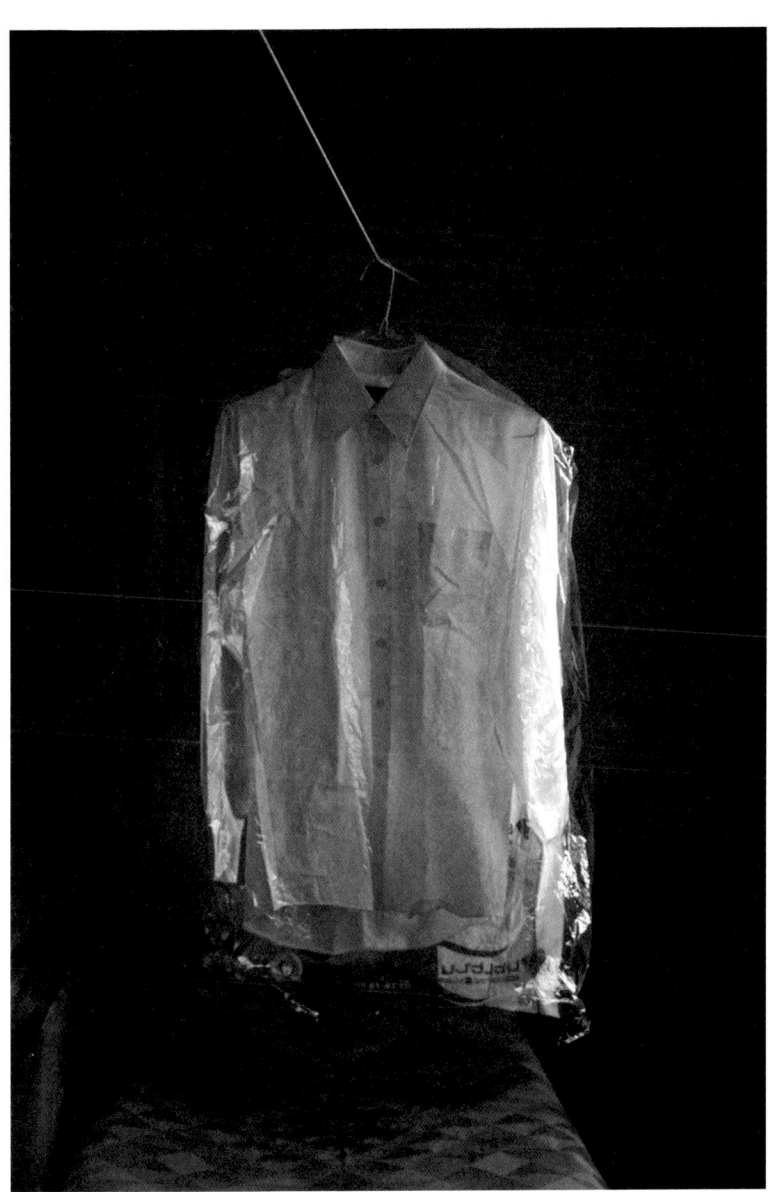

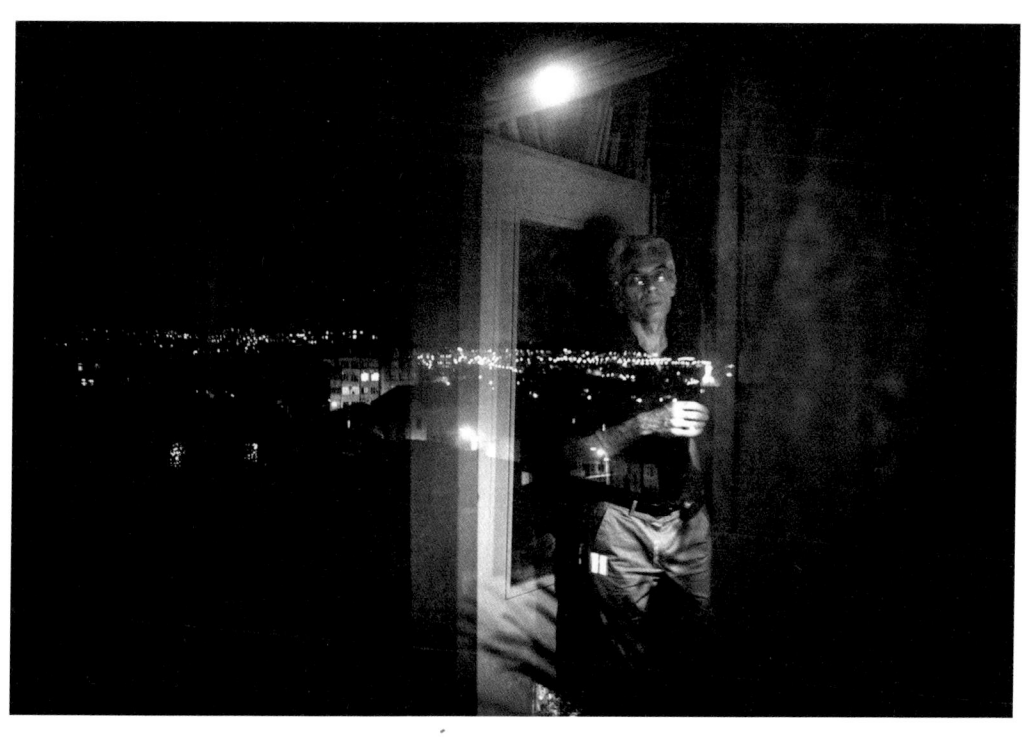

I keep searching for him.
I think I always will.

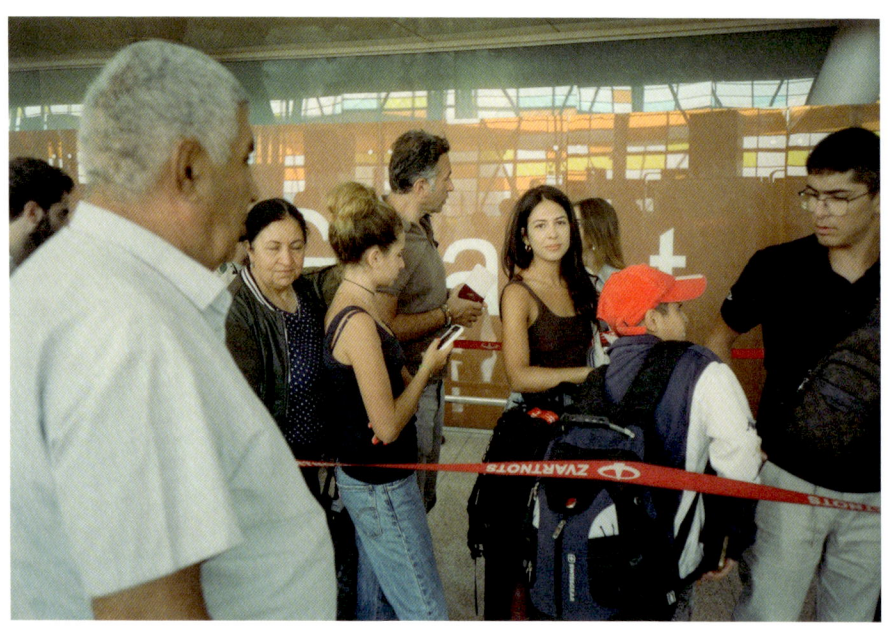

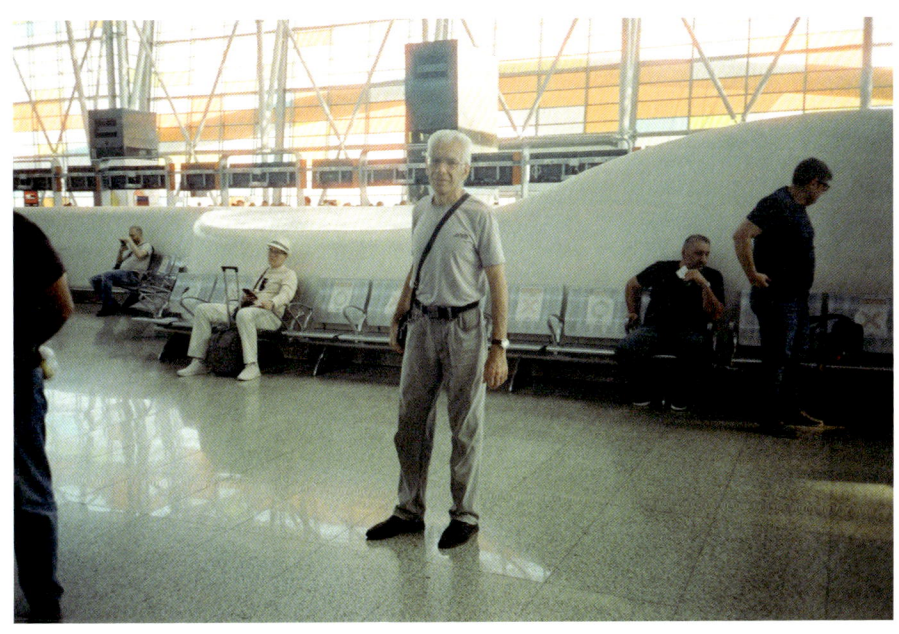

To my colleagues and friends
who supported me throughout the making of this book:

Rhiannon Adam
Julien Alamo
Jordan Alves
Daphne Angles
Rebecca Bengal
Phil Bicker
Emma Bowkett
Erin Brethauer
Adam Desiderio
Claartje van Dijk
Kate Emerson
James Estrin
David Feeney-Mosier
Galerie les Filles du Calvaire
Hannah Gottlieb-Graham
Clare Freestone
Amanda Hajjar
Ani Imnadze
Elizabeth Krist
Mike Lappin
Funa Maduka
Marie Magnier
Harut Mangasaryan
Marie Monteleone
Anne Perri
Zoe Potkin
Lizzie Presser
Fiona Rogers
Jeffrey Scales
Amy Singer
Nina Strochlic
Matt Stuart
Pauline Vermare
Clementine Williamson

To the teams at Atelier EXB and Aperture
for their support in creating this book.

And finally, my deepest gratitude
to my father.

Father
Photographs and text by Diana Markosian

Atelier EXB
Editor: Jordan Alves
Graphic design: Coline Aguettaz
Proofreading: Tom Ridgway
Production: Charlotte Debiolles, François Santerre
Color separation: Les Artisans du Regard, Paris
Partnerships: Yseult Chehata

Aperture
Project Editor: Richard Gregg
Proofreaders: Susan Ciccotti, Freddy Martinez

Additional staff of the Aperture book program includes:
Sarah Meister, Executive Director;
Michael Famighetti, Editor in Chief;
Sang Patten, Managing Editor, Books;
Caroline Foulke, Editorial Assistant;
Karina Eckmeier, Designer and Project Manager;
Minjee Cho, Production Director;
Andrea Chlad, Production Manager;
Thomas Bollier, Production Consultant;
Kellie McLaughlin, Director of Sales and Outreach;
Cansu Korkmaz, Sales and Operations Associate

First Aperture edition, 2024
Printed in Italy
10 9 8 7 6 5 4 3 2 1

Library of Congress Control Number: 2024943663
ISBN 978-1-59711-589-6

Copublished by Aperture and Atelier EXB.

To order Aperture books,
or inquire about gift or group orders, contact:
orders@aperture.org

For information about Aperture
trade distribution worldwide, visit:
aperture.org/distribution

aperture
548 West 28th Street, 4th Floor
New York, NY 10001
aperture.org

Aperture is a nonprofit publisher dedicated
to creating insight, community, and understanding
through photography.

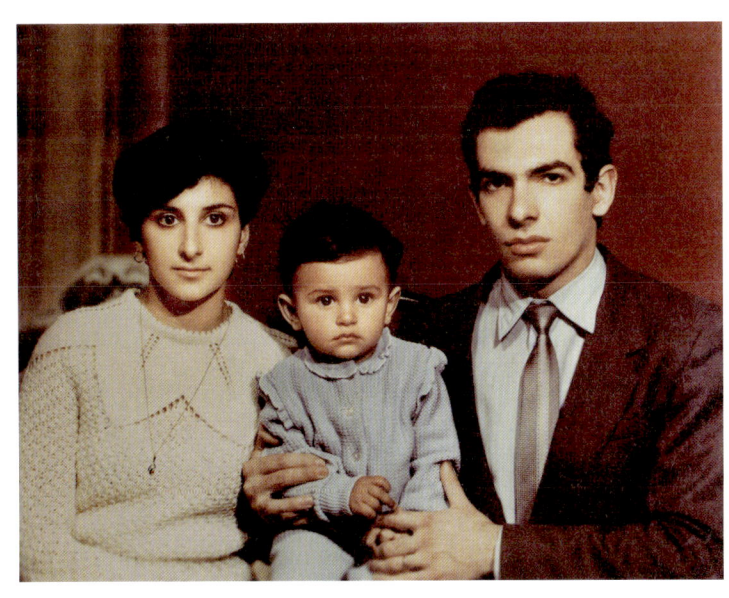

My father and I spent 15 years searching for each other.
He wrote hundreds of letters looking for me.
Who is missing from your life?

Use the attached envelope to write a letter.

Send to:
Aperture
548 West 28th Street, 4th Floor
New York, NY 10001
USA

Letters will be included as part
of a forthcoming exhibition by Diana Markosian.